PRINCIPLES OF PRODUCT MANAGEMENT

HOW TO LAND A PM JOB AND LAUNCH YOUR PRODUCT CAREER

PETER YANG

To Jenny and Serena for creating life's most meaningful memories.

CONTENTS

INTRODUCTION

It was late Saturday afternoon at Facebook's Building 20, a sprawling open office below a rooftop garden. Instead of enjoying my weekend, I stood in a windowless room practicing product management interview questions. A year ago, I had failed to pass the company's PM interview loop as an internal transfer, but this time, I thought to myself, it would be different.

It would be different because I had spent the past year growing a new Facebook app to millions of users and winning the support of a product director on my team. I just needed to pass the interviews, and the long hours I spent preparing for them would be worth it.

Interview day arrived, and I came out of the first two interviews feeling confident. I had built a good rapport with my interviewers and answered their product and execution questions well. Now it was time for the behavioral interview. I was ready to talk about how I successfully scaled the new Facebook app, but the first question caught me off guard: "Tell me about a time when you failed." I paused for a moment. *Calm down,* I thought to myself. *You already prepared a good answer to this question.* I gave my answer and shared more stories of failures and team conflicts with my interviewer over the next 45 minutes.

A few days passed with no response, and I began to feel anxious. Finally, on Friday afternoon, my product director stopped by my desk and asked if I had time to meet. We walked into that same windowless conference room. "Peter," she said, "You did well on two of the interviews, but your leadership examples weren't great. I'm afraid you didn't pass the loop." My heart sank. She tried to comfort me: "I know you did a great job over the past six months, and the team loves working with you. You could always try again in another year."

That was years ago. Since then, I've successfully transitioned to PM and launched many products at Amazon, Twitter, and other leading tech companies. I've also pursued my passion for helping the next generation of PMs succeed through training programs and mentorship. Through my experience and conversations with others, I've learned how tough it is to become a product manager and launch your product career.

This book is the guide that I wish I had when I first got started as a product manager. My goal is to give you the best practices on leading without authority, building a product, and landing a job all in one place.

What Do Product Managers Do?

Over the past decade, product management has become one of the most sought-after jobs in the U.S. Yet, few people outside the profession understand what PMs do. Those looking to enter the field often ask questions like "Do you need an MBA?", "Do you need to be technical?" and "Are product managers mini-CEOs?". To find answers, aspiring PMs need to sort through hundreds of blog posts or sign up for expensive boot camps.

A product manager's job is to lead their team to build products that solve their customer's most important problems. They do this by understanding the customer problem, identifying the right products to build, and executing with their team to bring the product to market.

How Is This Book Organized?

This book is a three-part, practical guide to help new and aspiring product managers land a PM job and launch their product career:

1. **Principles:** Part one covers the leadership principles that PMs use to lead their team to solve customer problems. Hear stories about how I learned these principles, often the hard way.
2. **Product development:** Part two covers how PMs at Facebook, Amazon, and other top companies build software products. We'll walk through the end-to-end product development process—from understanding the customer problem, to identifying the right product to build, to executing with your team to bring the product to market.
3. **Getting the job:** Part three covers how you can land a PM job and prepare for interviews with practice questions and answers from Facebook, Google, and more. We'll discuss the three most common types of PM interviews—product sense, execution, and behavioral—in depth.

Throughout this book, I've also included interviews with product leaders about their past successes and failures and what they wish they had known when they started their PM careers.

Let's start with the most important topic: the core principles that will help you lead without authority as a product manager.

PART I

PRINCIPLES

What skills do great product managers have? Are they technical wizards, analytical machines, or product visionaries? These skills are important, but by far the most critical skill is leadership. Great product managers rely on their leadership skills every day to help their team ship products that solve customer problems.

Product managers build leadership skills through adversity. When your product fails to gain traction, when your team falls apart, or when your manager gives you tough feedback— these are all opportunities to become a better PM and person.

Part one of this book outlines six principles that I think define great PMs and the stories that led me to them.

1

TAKE OWNERSHIP

"Your first project is to launch our new credit card marketplace. This project should be straightforward because we already defined the product and you just need to get it shipped."

In early 2019, I joined Credit Karma to grow the credit card business —the largest revenue stream for the company. The team had worked for months on a complete redesign of the cards marketplace for logged out users, and my job was to get it out the door.

I caught up with my teammates who led the redesign. They shared that one of the goals was to make it easier for people to browse cards by category (e.g., travel cards, cash back cards, etc.). The team had conducted user research to identify this customer need, so I didn't question it. Over the next few weeks, I helped everyone get the new marketplace ready for launch.

Launch day arrived, and we celebrated with cupcakes. We rolled out the new marketplace to 50% of users as a test, and everyone felt confident that it would perform better than the old one.

Unfortunately, the numbers told a different story. As the days passed, a sense of dread crept over me. The new marketplace was performing worse, far worse. A week after launch, revenue was down 10% for the new marketplace compared to the old one.

I started making excuses in my head. "I didn't define this product, so it's not my fault." "I'm new to the team and don't want to rock the boat." "Maybe if we wait another week, the numbers will improve."

But instead of making excuses or blaming others, I knew I had to take ownership. I told my manager, "This is my fault, and I will fix this. We're looking at the numbers now to understand what went wrong." Over the next few days, I dove into the data and discussed the problem with my teammates. We realized that most people visited the marketplace after searching for "best cards" on Google. Unlike the people we recruited for user research, our real customers wanted to shop for cards right away. A quick look at our competitors' websites confirmed our hypothesis: All of them displayed a list of best cards directly on their marketplace.

With this insight, I asked the team to show cards directly on the page and highlight the key benefits of each card. It took a few more tests, but we went from a -10% revenue dip to a +10% revenue lift and were finally able to release the product.

By taking ownership of the initial failure, I built trust with my team and my manager. By being the first to admit my mistake, I encouraged my teammates to take ownership as well.

PRINCIPLE #1: **Take Ownership.**

Be Humble

Taking ownership starts with being humble. As a product manager, you succeed or fail through your team.

When your team runs into a problem, it's easy to blame others or make excuses. Instead, be the first to admit how you contributed to the problem and what you're doing to address it. When other people see you lead with your mistakes, they're more likely to share their mistakes and focus on solving the problem as well.

When your team achieves a new milestone, it's easy to take credit for it. Instead, give as much credit as possible to your team. Build trust with your teammates by recognizing them in public and showing genuine appreciation in 1:1s.

Control Negative Emotions

Take ownership of your emotions. It's natural to get emotional when you're in a heated debate with a teammate or receiving critical feedback from your manager. But people don't make good decisions when they're emotional. Think about it this way: When something goes wrong, would you rather work with someone who is calm or someone who is raising their voice? As a product manager, you must check your ego and control your negative emotions.

Controlling your emotions is easier said than done, so here are a few tips:

1. Recognize the warning signs when you're getting emotional, such as your face getting flustered.
2. Take a breath and listen to the other person's point of view.
3. Reflect for a few seconds, then respond in a clear, calm manner.

Practice these steps all the time. If you can get good at controlling your emotions, it'll make being a product manager much less stressful.

Build Relationships

Take ownership of your relationships. Building relationships is just as important as owning a list of tasks because your hardest tasks require collaboration and alignment with other people.

To build relationships, check your ego, and put yourself in other people's shoes. Keep them updated on your project's progress. Listen when they're speaking, and show empathy for their perspectives. Help them out and expect nothing in return. Product managers that have an attitude of "I did this for you, so you owe me one" don't go very far.

If you're humble, collaborative, and genuine, you'll soon develop great relationships with people who will be eager to work with you.

2

PRIORITIZE AND EXECUTE

It was January, and I had just returned to work after a relaxing winter break. To my surprise, my engineering manager told me that he was leaving the team to try something new. At the same time, we faced an aggressive deadline to migrate a customer dashboard to a new code base—clean-up work that none of my engineers wanted to do.

I felt overwhelmed. But instead of not doing anything, I took action. I made a list of priorities and focused on the most important priority first.

My engineers weren't going to stay if they didn't have an engineering manager, so recruiting was at the top of my list. I drafted job requirements, engaged recruiters, and asked for referrals. After a few weeks of moonlighting as a recruiter, I found a great engineering manager for the team.

Next, I needed to understand why my engineers weren't excited about the dashboard project. "This dashboard has a poor user experience, and our customers complain about it every day," they explained. "Migrating it to a new code base won't fix these problems." They were right. I had put too much emphasis on meeting an arbitrary deadline set by executives instead of addressing the real customer problem. With my team's support, I convinced management to give us an extra month to make improvements to the dashboard as part of the migration.

My engineers were now excited to get to work, but I had a new problem. Even with an extra month, I realized that we would still struggle to get the migration completed in time. Luckily, I had built relationships with other teams whose products relied on the dashboard. I convinced them to lend engineers to help with the migration since the dashboard also served as a platform for their products.

By prioritizing and executing on the above, I kept my team together and shipped a new dashboard that customers loved.

———

IN YOUR PM CAREER, you will face a similar situation. There will be multiple things to work on, and you'll feel overwhelmed. Which brings us to our second principle:

PRINCIPLE #2: **Prioritize and Execute.**

Focus

It's better to achieve a breakthrough in a single goal than to pursue multiple goals at once.

Every morning, identify no more than three tasks that you want to accomplish during the day. Update your calendar to reflect these priorities and say no to all non-essential work.

During the day, you might receive an urgent request that isn't on your priority list. Understand if this request is both urgent and important because many urgent requests are interruptions that don't help you achieve your goals. Figure out what matters and focus on doing that well, don't waste your time on anything else.

Communicate Your Priorities

Just as important as knowing which priorities to focus on, is communicating your priorities to others. This way, everyone has shared goals and expectations.

It's especially important to make sure that you're aligned on priorities with your manager and your team. Use your weekly 1:1 with your manager to align on the top three tasks that you want to accomplish during the week. Similarly, use your weekly team meeting and daily stand-ups to align with your team on what the most important tasks are.

Do Whatever It Takes

Once you, your team, and your manager share the same priorities, you must do whatever it takes to accomplish them. Whether it's entering data, testing your product for bugs, or aligning with another team on a dependency, no task is too menial or trivial for you as a product manager.

3

START WITH WHY

In the room were the CEO and his executive team. All eyes were on me. Everyone wanted to hear about a new analytics product that my team was building.

I felt confident. I started the meeting by sharing the product designs and conveying all the great insights that we were going to deliver to customers.

As I walked through my presentation, I didn't pay attention to the CEO's body language. People told me afterward that he was becoming agitated. After about 15 minutes, he suddenly blurted out: "I use Google Analytics to drill down on data all the time, and I don't see powerful drill-down tools in what you're building."

This question caught me off guard. I tried to explain that our customers didn't want to drill down on data, but my CEO was hearing none of it. Later, I found out that he had spent a lot of time using Google Analytics to drill down on data when the company was still a start-up. As a result, he believed that customers wanted to do the same thing. Instead, user research showed that many of our customers didn't have time to drill down on data after a long day at work. The goal of the new analytics product was to "give customers a list of actions that they can take to grow their business at a glance."

Unfortunately, I didn't start the meeting by explaining this goal and sharing the supporting user research. Since I didn't align with my CEO on the customer problem before diving into the solution, it was now very difficult for him to listen to my explanation. I could have avoided a lot of confusion by aligning on the why (the goal) with him first.

———

THE MAJORITY of disagreements happen when people are not aligned on the why. Aligning on the why can help you avoid:

- Building a product when your team doesn't know why they're building it.
- Sharing data with executives when they don't know why the data matters.
- Arguing about a product design when no one knows why the product matters to the customer.

Always get aligned on the why early, it's one of the best time investments that you can make.

PRINCIPLE #3: Start with Why.

Obsess Over the Customer Problem

As a product manager, your most important why is the customer problem that your product is trying to solve. Include your team and other stakeholders in understanding the customer problem and selecting the right goal metric to grow. This way, everyone can contribute, feel ownership, and stay motivated to solve the problem even if the product changes.

Communicate Why Constantly

Once you've aligned on the why with your team, you need to communicate it regularly to everyone. It may seem redundant to remind people about the customer problem and goal all the time, but this constant communication achieves two objectives. First, it helps everyone internalize the why so they can make decisions with the same goal in mind. Second, if people are not aligned on the why, they're more likely to bring up objections if you talk about it constantly.

Keep It Simple

When communicating with others, the most critical question that you need to answer is, "Do people understand?" If people don't understand the why, they won't be able to execute.

Keep your communication simple, short, and specific. Check to see if people understand your message by asking them to explain it back to you. Encourage them to ask questions if they're not aligned so that you can discover the truth together.

4

FIND THE TRUTH

"Of all the features that you can cut, We can't believe that you want to cut a safety feature!"

The Twitch safety team wasn't happy. They were responsible for making Twitch a safe video platform for creators and viewers to interact around live streams. We were reviewing raids, a new product that would allow any creator to send their viewers to another creator's channel. During beta testing, most creators used raids to help each other grow. However, in a few cases, creators raided each other to throw insults and abuse.

The safety team was mad because I wanted to cut a feature that would allow creators to shut down abusive raids. My rationale was simple—there were already existing safety tools that creators could use to manage raids and we needed to cut something to meet our launch date.

I listened to the safety team's argument. "Yes, it might be true that 99% of raids are good," they said, "but the 1% of raids that are bad are some of the worst experiences that people can have on our platform." I started to think about the worst-case outcome: We ship this product, and people abuse it on day one. Even if creators can shut down this abuse with existing tools, building better tools will show the community that we cared about protecting them against bad behavior. I realized that the safety team was right.

I said, "You're right, we can't cut the safety feature. But can we work together to design a simpler solution that will still allow us to meet our ship date?" Suddenly, the meeting became very productive. We worked on simplifying the solution, and the safety team even agreed to help build it. A few weeks later, we launched raids on stage at Twitch's annual creator conference and made safety our primary message. Our community loved that we built safety tools on day one.

———

WHEN YOU GET into disagreements with others, remember that your job as a product manager is to find the truth, not to be right all the time.

Because people expect PMs to know everything about their product, I used to spend hours looking at customer research and crafting a polished document before sharing it with anyone. I would then go into a meeting with a goal to convince everyone else to see things my way. This approach is inefficient.

It's inefficient because no matter how much preparation I do, there's always a chance that I could be wrong. So instead of going into a discussion with a goal of "How can I convince this person to see things my way?" I now have a goal of "How can we discover the truth together?"

PRINCIPLE #4: Find the Truth.

Seek Knowledgeable People

The fastest way to find the truth is to seek knowledgeable people who are willing to disagree. Knowledgeable people could include your customers, your teammates, or anyone with relevant experience. After you form an initial opinion about a decision, find others to debate the decision. During these debates, identify significant unknowns together ("How do we know that users want this?") and follow-up on these unknowns as quickly as possible to find an answer.

With the help of other knowledgeable people, you'll quickly find questions you've missed or holes in your logic. If you're wrong about something, admit it early. There's no shame in changing your mind to get closer to the truth.

Balance Decision Quality with Decision Speed

Even with the help of other knowledgeable people, you'll likely won't have all the information that you need to make a decision. It's useful to think of decisions as one-way or two-way doors. Two-way doors are decisions that can be easily reversed, so prioritize decision speed even if you don't have perfect information. One-way doors are rarer. These decisions are hard to change, so try to gather more information if you're uncertain.

Disagree and Commit

Every decision has two phases: 1) gather and debate; and 2) commit and execute. During the first phase, if you genuinely believe that the decision is wrong and have the evidence to back it up, then disagree openly. It's always easier to compromise with the decision-maker to avoid damaging a relationship, especially if that person is your manager or an executive. But your goal should be to find the truth no matter what, even when doing so is uncomfortable.

After a decision is made, you must commit yourself and your team to execute on it. Even if you don't agree with the decision, it's your job to make sure you understand the rationale behind the decision and explain that to your team. It's never acceptable to say, "Because my boss said so."

We'll dive into decision making more in part two of this book.

5

___

BE RADICALLY TRANSPARENT

A few years ago, I worked with a data scientist who wanted to transition to product management. We invited her to work on my team for a few months as a trial run.

As her mentor, I wanted to know why she wanted to be a product manager and how I could help her succeed. She mentioned that she had a lot of great product ideas but wanted to get better at presenting them to others.

Over the next few weeks, I found opportunities for her to present to engineers, partner teams, and executives. After each presentation, I shared what I thought she did well and where she could improve. Slowly but surely, she gained the confidence needed to present her product ideas more effectively.

However, I saw a more pressing issue that my colleague needed to work on—being comfortable with ambiguity. As a data scientist, she shared her work only after she was 100% confident about it. As a result, it took her a long time to deliver product requirement documents (PRDs), which was starting to block the rest of the team.

I brought up the issue with her: "I notice that you're taking a long time to finish your PRDs. Is there anything I can do to help?" "I just need to look at a few more metrics to validate my assumptions," she explained. I offered my feedback: "Sharing the PRD early and often empowers the rest of your team to contribute ideas. I also wanted to write the perfect PRDs early in my career before I realized that collaborating with others was the fastest way to build the best product."

Although my feedback was candid, she responded well because she knew that I cared about her success. We decided to meet for a few minutes every day so that I could help her polish her PRDs. It wasn't easy, but eventually, she became more comfortable with ambiguity and was able to transition to product management successfully.

This story illustrates our fifth principle:

Principle #5: Be Radically Transparent.

Many people have written books about radical transparency, but the best framework that I've found is from the book *Radical Candor* by Kim Scott. Kim recommends that you measure radical transparency on two axes: how often you care personally, and how often you challenge directly.

Care Personally

Caring personally is about investing in other people's success:

1. At least once a month, find time for real 1:1 conversations with your teammates. Seek to understand their goals and offer to help in any way.
2. If people ask you for advice, share personal stories, and show vulnerability. Be genuine about your past failures and mistakes and what you learned from them.
3. If people are doing a great job, praise them both publicly and

privately. Call out specific examples of things they did well and make sure that other people can see it, too.

If you build caring relationships with people, they will be much more likely to listen to you when you deliver constructive feedback.

Challenge Directly

Challenging directly is about giving constructive feedback effectively:

1. Deliver feedback as soon as possible. For example, if your teammate ran a meeting that didn't have clear next steps, pull her aside and provide feedback when the meeting is still fresh in her mind.
2. Give specific examples in your feedback. For example, you could say to the same teammate: "You discussed a few next steps in the meeting, but I think people are confused about who is responsible for each task. Next time, it could help if you wrote the steps down on the whiteboard and assigned owners before the meeting ended."
3. Make your feedback about the work, not the person. For example, the above feedback is much more helpful than telling your teammate: "I think you could work on running better meetings."

As Kim describes: "Be humble, helpful, offer guidance in person and immediately, praise in public, criticize in private, and don't personalize."[1]

Empower Others

One way to measure your success as a PM is how successful your team is without you. If everyone on your team is executing well even when you're not there, then you're probably doing a good job.

How do you empower other people on your team to lead? First, you need to make sure that they understand why the product they're building matters to customers. Then, you need to set up the right processes to enable them to execute efficiently. When everyone on your team understands the why and can prioritize and execute without you, you'll have more time to think about long-term strategy instead of worrying about daily execution. Everyone wins.

6

BE HONEST WITH YOURSELF

"Your bias for action too often comes across as impatience. This manifests in the form of curt behavior in meetings and dismissiveness of other people's ideas."

Early in my product management career, this feedback from my manager hit me like a ton of bricks. I had always taken pride in my ability to get things done and deliver products ahead of schedule. How could my bias for action lead to a negative performance review?

After a few days of soul searching, I realized that my manager was right. I was so focused on moving fast that my teammates felt left behind. For example, I would reach out to partners directly without consulting my partner manager, which left her feeling demoralized. By not consulting experts like her, I was not only damaging my relationships with my teammates but also doing a disservice to the product.

The directness of the feedback was a wake-up call for me to improve. I worked hard to earn back the trust that I had lost with my team. A year later, the feedback that I received was completely different:

"You listen to everyone to make the product better and take people's feedback to heart. Even if you disagree, you document the different viewpoints and the rationale. People respect that you have low ego, a lot of patience, and take time to understand different trade-offs."

So, what changed? My bias for action was a strength that turned into a weakness when I started using it as an excuse to be impatient with my teammates. Only after receiving blunt feedback and making a genuine effort to improve did I recover.

To lead others as a product manager, you first need to lead yourself. Since you have no real authority over anyone as a PM, you'll only succeed if people want to work with you. That's why great product managers are honest with themselves and have a growth mindset. They are constantly looking for ways to improve by setting goals, reflecting on progress, and seeking constructive feedback.

Principle #6: Be Honest with Yourself.

Set Clear Goals

Setting long-term goals helps you focus on what truly matters to you. Like product goals, your personal goals should have clear success criteria and time constraints. For example, your goals might be to "transition to PM in a year" or "get positive feedback on collaboration from colleagues in my next performance review." Although these goals should rarely change, you should be flexible about how you achieve them when new opportunities or challenges arise.

For example, my goal was to transition from product marketing to product management. To achieve this goal, I prioritized learning skills from other product managers over making progress in my marketing career. My plan, however, wasn't flexible enough. I focused too much on transitioning internally at my company that I didn't consider external options. Only after I became more open to external opportunities did I finally make the transition.

Reflect Often

As you make progress toward your goals, you'll experience both successes and setbacks. When these events occur, you must reflect to identify your strengths and weaknesses.

When you reach a milestone like launching a new product or moving a goal metric, reflect on what strengths helped you along the way. These strengths are usually activities that you're both good at and enjoy doing. For example, you may excel in execution and can balance multiple projects at ease. Or you may be an excellent mediator whom people rely to resolve conflicts. Whatever your strengths are, you should find opportunities to use them as frequently as possible.

When you experience a setback like failing to resolve a team conflict or receiving a negative performance review, reflect on what weaknesses led to it. Based on my experience, people usually have one significant weakness that's a common thread through most of their past setbacks. For example, I struggle with being impatient. My impatience has surfaced in past mistakes like becoming frustrated with colleagues or leaving good jobs too early. Whatever your weaknesses are, you must stay vigilant and keep working on them.

Seek Feedback from Others

After you've had a chance to reflect on your strengths and weaknesses, you should validate them with people you trust. It may feel awkward to ask others for feedback, but the earlier you know what they think about you, the sooner you can take steps to improve. Here are a few ways to ask for feedback:

- After an important meeting, pull a teammate aside and ask: "How do you think that meeting went? What did I do well, and what could I have done better?"
- After working together with a teammate, ask: "Now that

we've spent some time together, I'd love to understand how I can be a better partner for you."

If you're aware of your strengths and weaknesses and actively seek constructive feedback from others, then you're well on your way to becoming a great product manager.

7

INTERVIEW: SHARMEEN BROWAREK CHAPP

Sharmeen is the VP of the Viewer Engagement at Twitch, a live streaming platform owned by Amazon. In this interview, she describes her product management journey, overcoming challenging situations, and evaluating PMs.

Can you describe your journey to product management after college?

My first job after college was at Hewlett-Packard as an engineer working on fabricating circuit boards. It was the typical Electrical Engineering job, but I felt unfulfilled. I wanted to level up to see the bigger picture instead of getting stuck in the details.

The 2008 recession hit, so I went back to school to get my masters. After that, I joined Raytheon to work on missile integration for the defense industry. There, I became a manager for the first time. I remember feeling terrified because I was managing people twice my age. But it turned out that people enjoyed having me as a manager because they saw that I cared. I spent a lot of time listening to their career aspirations and tried my best to give them what they needed to succeed.

I think that's a key lesson for product managers as well: Spend time to get to know your team on a personal level, and show that you care about them. It goes a long way.

How did you transition to product?

After four years at Raytheon, I realized that I had been living in Boston for ten years. I wanted to move back to California to be part of the tech industry. I ended up joining as a senior product engineer at a start-up. Since it was a start-up, I was wearing multiple hats—from building the company's quality assurance processes to driving product launches.

Working at the start-up exposed me to what product managers do. I realized that transitioning to product manager was a chicken and egg problem because companies typically won't consider you for the role unless you already have product management experience. Back then, I felt like the only way to break in was to either to join an associate product management program, get an MBA, or try to transfer internally at a company. I remember it was hard to convince companies to even talk to me despite my years of experience as an engineer and manager.

Thankfully, the recruiter who hired me at the start-up encouraged me to apply to Twitch. I got connected to a senior director there who put me through the hiring process. I convinced Twitch that I was taking a risk on them by becoming an individual contributor instead of a manager, just like they were taking a risk on me by hiring me as a product manager with no product experience.

What do you do at Twitch?

I'm the VP of the Viewer Engagement team. Our mission is to help creators build thriving communities on Twitch and our products include chat, safety, moderation, and more. It's been rewarding to grow from an individual contributor to leading not just a product team but also engineering, design, and data science.

Can you give me an example of a tough situation that you faced in the past?

A few years ago, I worked on a new initiative with a small, scrappy team of five people. We did market research and identified what we thought was a huge opportunity for Twitch. However, when we presented our ideas to executives, we just kept hitting a wall. It felt like every conversation we were having, we just weren't on the same page.

I remember feeling very demoralized. Eventually, when I sat down to think about the root cause of the problem, I realized that the company wasn't ready yet to tackle this opportunity. Our executives were focused on running the core business well, so they didn't have a lot of resources to allocate to new initiatives.

The fundamental disconnect was that we were not aligned on goals and priorities with the executive team. After we realized this, we shifted the team to work on something that was more immediately pressing for the company.

Even though the project got shut down, it came as a relief to the team because it was much easier to work on something that aligned with business objectives than to fight an uphill battle.

What I realized through this process is that you have to think about how the work you're doing ties back to the company's strategic goals. You also need to share and evangelize your ideas early and often to reach alignment.

Can you give me an example of how you managed multiple stakeholders on a project?

A year into Twitch I worked on a project to redesign the channel page that viewers used to watch streams. This page is critical to the entire company, so everyone wanted to be involved. In the past, multiple product managers had tried to redesign the page but failed because they couldn't agree on what to change.

The pressure was high, but I came at it with the perspective that it's not about what I think the channel page should look like. Instead, I focused everyone on the problems we wanted to solve for the customer. I also included all stakeholders in brainstorming sessions and debates to get closer to the truth.

Did it take a lot of effort to get stakeholders aligned?

Yes, I remember having the same meeting with multiple stakeholders (design, engineering, etc.) to walk them through the user problem, the goal of the project, and our design. I spent a lot of time in these meetings listening to and documenting their feedback. Even if I disagreed with their feedback, I still wrote it down and attempted to explain to them why we were not prioritizing their asks.

This process took a long time and many meetings but it was worth it to get people aligned.

Other than meeting with stakeholders did you use any other tactics?

Well, I think it was a mix of 1:1s, large group meetings, and constant e-mail updates. The key is to be as inclusive as possible. I remember inviting everyone and sending notes after each meeting. I also think it's important to listen more in these meetings than speak. You want to get stakeholders to express their feedback. The more feedback and perspectives you get, the closer you can get to building a great product. Finally, I think it's important to hold these meetings with the mindset that everyone has the same intentions and just wants to build the right product for customers. We're all coming from a good place, wanting to build something great; if you focus on that attitude, the rest of the pieces usually fall into place.

How do you evaluate product managers on your team?

Holistically. Product management is a unique role where we manage by influence. Every part of the process matters. From great communication, teamwork, inclusivity, to execution skills.

How do you deliver feedback to product managers on your team?

I'm very rational when I deliver feedback. First, I try to understand the other person's side of the story first. Next, I try to deliver my feedback with specific examples. I say something like "This happened, which caused this subsequent action, and then affected people in this way." Structuring the feedback with the facts first before the emotional element makes it easier for people to understand. Finally, after delivering the feedback, I work with the person to discuss what actionable improvements we can make. As a manager, I think I have to keep pushing until I see the person grow or change their response.

Do you have any mentors who have really helped you in your product management career? How did you find them?

I thought about the skills that I wanted to develop and then found people who I felt excelled in those skills. Then I just asked.

What traits define good product managers?

I like product managers who have a sense of positive energy. Because product management is about leading by influence, you want someone who radiates positivity. At the end of a project, people should have the perspective of "I want to build another product with PM because it was an awesome experience." Personally, I find it helpful to be a relentless optimist. Even if I'm low in energy, I still try to be positive. On the days when I feel down, I notice that people feel it. The more senior you become, the more you have to lead by example.

I also think great product managers are very inclusive and collaborative. As a PM, your main job is to advocate for the customer. If you always come from that point, it takes the emotions or need to be defensive out of debates.

Finally, I think good product managers have an ownership mindset. They hold themselves accountable, have high standards, and do whatever it takes to help their team succeed.

Any parting words of wisdom for new or aspiring product managers?

Hmm...there are a lot of don'ts: Don't let the hiring process discourage you. Don't let impostor syndrome get the best of you. Don't get over-whelmed by it all. But it's better to focus on the positives. Have faith in yourself! Be humble, advocate for your customer, and you'll be great!

8

INTERVIEW: AMEET RANADIVE

Ameet is the Chief Product Officer of GetYourGuide, a travel company based in Europe. In this interview, he describes how he evaluates product managers, how PMs can build trust with others, and how they can accelerate their careers.

You've managed product teams at Twitter, Instagram, and now GetYourGuide. At a high level, how do you evaluate product managers?

I look for three things when evaluating product managers: Vision, Execution, and Leadership.

One of the most important things that product managers do is to develop a compelling product vision. To develop a vision, you need to answer questions like: What problem are you solving for customers? How is your solution better than the customers' alternatives? What is distinct and innovative about your approach? You have to deeply understand customer needs, question defaults, and have a beginner's mind.

Vision alone is not enough to have an impact, product managers also must be able to execute and get things done. Two important factors for execution are defining the product and making effective decisions. To define the product, PMs must select the right output (impact) metric and prioritize features by the output metric. In addition, they must simplify their products as much as possible, and take an iterative, hypothesis-driven approach.

The final responsibility of a product management is leadership. Products are built by teams, and teams look to the product manager for guidance. To help teams persist through setbacks, PMs must have a growth mindset and demonstrate resilience and grit. PMs can build trust by operating as givers (not takers), and by creating credibility for themselves through integrity, intent, capabilities, and results. Finally, PMs have to sell their ideas and their team's contributions with excellent communication and persuasion skills.

How can product managers effectively build trust with others and improve their leadership skills?

I think Steve Covey's book *The Speed of Trust* tackles this question well. Covey provides four cores to build trust: 1) Integrity; 2) Intent; 3) Capabilities; and 4) Results.

Integrity is about being honest and showing humility. The moment someone questions whether you are honest, their trust in you nosedives. Be humble and open-minded to the ideas and perspectives of others. Act with courage: Stand up for your beliefs and do the right thing, even when it's difficult.

Intent is about motives and behavior. You have to genuinely care about others, seek mutually beneficial outcomes, and then act in the interests of others. It's helpful to declare your intent to signal your motivation and to be transparent about your agenda.

Capabilities are your talents and knowledge for the task at hand. To be viewed as capable, play from your strengths, improve your attitudes, and continually develop your skills and knowledge.

Finally, you must produce results. To do that well, take responsibility for results (especially negative ones), expect to win, finish strong, and communicate your results.

How can people make progress in their product management career?

Great question. Based on my own experience and the experiences of others, I've come to think about PM career progress in five steps:

1. **Nail the work you have been given.** You have to build trust with your management and your teammates that you are someone who can deliver solid results. Clarify the expectations for your role, and then work hard and work smart to deliver those results.

2. **Look for more high impact work.** This "extra credit" work cannot come at the cost of continuing to perform on your "day job." You have to continue nailing your original responsibilities and the additional ones.

3. **Develop a vision for your area.** Create the space for yourself to stick your head up, look ahead (for the long-term perspective) and look around (for the broader awareness). Become a thought partner for your teammates and for your manager, so that they start to see you as a trusted advisor and, in the case of your teammates, as a mentor.

4. **Make yourself redundant.** If you can find someone to take on your original responsibilities, it frees you up to take on additional scope. Sometimes the opportunities for additional responsibilities come through a "lucky break" in the organization. If you have your own successor at the moment that a "lucky break" presents itself, you will be more attractive for management to entrust with the opportunity.

5. **Put yourself in high-growth situations.** Finally, in addition to all of the things above, put yourself into high-growth situations and companies. In these high-growth environments, there is a lot more white space to take initiative; there will naturally be more "lucky break"

opportunities; and it will be easier to attract and find your own successor.

Even with all of the tips above, it's important to remember that promotions will require patience and luck. Don't sweat it if you get passed over for a promotion this time around; keep playing the long game, do great work and build great relationships, and the promotions and recognition will come over time.

PART II

PRODUCT DEVELOPMENT

Product managers build products that solve customer problems and help their company grow. They do this by following the "understand, identify, and execute" product development loop.

Part two of this book walks through this product development loop in detail. First, you need to understand the customer problem and how it relates to your company's goals. Next, you need to identify the right products to build with your team. This step involves crafting an inspiring mission, vision, and strategy; creating a roadmap with clear OKRs (objectives and key results); and writing detailed product requirements. Finally, you need to execute efficiently with your team to ship the product. This step requires excellent project management, communication, and decision-making skills.

Let's start by reviewing this product development loop at a high level.

9

PRODUCT DEVELOPMENT LOOP

Every company approaches product development differently. Some companies are chaotic and don't have a process at all. Other companies have a process with too many steps that slow down the pace of shipping.

My favorite process is the "understand, identify, and execute" loop. This loop has three phases:

1. **Understand**: What is the customer problem that we want to solve?
2. **Identify**: What product should we build to solve the problem?
3. **Execute**: What is the most efficient way to get the product shipped?

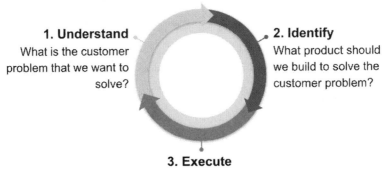

1. Understand
What is the customer
problem that we want to
solve?

2. Identify
What product should
we build to solve the
customer problem?

3. Execute
What is the most efficient way to get the product shipped?

Figure 1. *The "understand, identify, and execute" product development loop.*

Let's use an analogy to illustrate how this loop works. Suppose that you're going on a fishing trip at a nearby lake. First, you need to understand if the lake has fish. Next, you need to identify the right gear to bring in order to catch the fish. Finally, you need to execute by casting your line, waiting for a fish to take the bait, and reeling in your catch. If you miss any step—such as fishing at a lake that doesn't have fish or forgetting to bring your gear—you'll be out of luck.

Developing products is like catching fish, with one key difference. As a product manager, you're not building products alone. Instead, your job is to work through the "understand, identify, and execute" loop with your team.

Understand: What Is the Customer Problem That We Want to Solve?

Your goal in the understand phase is to craft a problem statement that answer three questions:

1. What is the customer problem?
2. How do we know that this problem exists?
3. Why is it critical that we solve this problem?

This is the most critical phase of product development because many products fail by not solving a real customer problem. Start with a team brainstorm to understand everyone's intuitions on the biggest problems that your customers face. Then, evaluate whether these problems exist by talking to customers, looking at user research, and analyzing metrics. Finally, prioritize the problems that will have the biggest impact on growing your team's goal metric.

You want to get your team invested in the why (the problem and the goal) first before tackling the solution. We'll discuss the understand phase more starting with the Customer Problem chapter.

Identify: What Product Should We Build to Solve the Problem?

Your goal in the identify phase is to define a product that will solve the customer problem that you've prioritized with your team.

The identify phase starts with defining an overall mission, vision, and strategy to give everyone on your team a shared purpose, an idea of what success looks like, and a plan to get there. After aligning on the strategy, you need to break it down into an actionable roadmap with objectives and key results. Finally, you need to define each product in your roadmap by writing product requirements and press releases.

We'll dive into the identify phase starting with the Mission, Vision, and Strategy chapter.

Execute: What Is the Most Efficient Way to Get the Product Shipped?

Your goal in the execute phase is to help your team ship the product you've defined as efficiently as possible. Great execution requires excellent project management, communication, and decision-making skills.

We'll dive into the execute phase starting with the Project Management chapter.

Why Is "Understand, Identify, and Execute" a Loop?

"Understand, identify, and execute" is a loop because your job is never done. After shipping a product, you need to go back to the understand phase to determine if the product addressed the customer problem and moved the goal metric. Each pass through the loop is a chance for your team to get better at understanding the problem, identifying the solution, and executing to bring the product to market.

Now that we covered the loop at a high level, let's dive into the first phase of product development—understanding the customer problem.

10

UNDERSTANDING THE CUSTOMER PROBLEM

Amazon has a famous obsession: "Start with the customer and work backward." But how does this actually work?

As Jeff Bezos describes:[1]

> The #1 thing that has made us successful by far is an obsessive-compulsive focus on the customer as opposed to the competitor.
>
> There are many advantages to a customer-centric approach, but here's the big one: customers are always beautifully, wonderfully dissatisfied, even when they report being happy and business is great. Customers always want something better, and your desire to delight customers will drive you to invent on their behalf.

To understand the customer problem, you need to answer three questions:

1. What is the customer problem?
2. How do we know that this problem exists?
3. Why is it critical that we solve this problem?

What Is the Customer Problem?

Understanding the problems that your customers face is very much an exercise in empathy. Start by researching who your customers are and putting yourself in their shoes. What is your customer trying to accomplish? What's on her mind, and how is she feeling? What's the underlying problem?

Rather than work on these questions by yourself, hold a team brainstorm to collect everyone's intuitions about the customer. During the brainstorm, check to see if people feel an emotional connection to the customer. You'll know you're on the right track when your team feels the customer's pain and wants badly to help. Here are notes from a sample brainstorm meeting about a customer problem:

Who is the customer?

Jane is a working mom with two kids at home.

What is the customer trying to accomplish?

She just finished work and needs to buy groceries to cook dinner for her family.

What is the customer journey?

1. Leave work

Feeling: Tired, anxious, rushed.

Thinking: Grocery store is far, worried about traffic, wants to be healthy and save money.

Doing: Finding the closest grocery store and driving or walking there from work.

2. Buy groceries

Feeling: Tired, anxious, rushed.

Thinking: Kids must be hungry, can't decide which groceries to buy.

<u>Doing</u>: Walking the aisles to find groceries, waiting in line at check out.

3. Cook dinner

<u>Feeling</u>: Tired, relieved, resentful.

<u>Thinking</u>: Why can't my husband cook? Hope this tastes good.

<u>Doing</u>: Cooking, cleaning up kitchen.

What is the underlying customer problem?

Today, working professionals don't have the time or mental energy to shop for groceries and prepare healthy meals.

Figure 2. *Visualize what your customer is thinking, feeling, and doing to identify their underlying problem.*

When crafting the problem statement as a team, avoid these pitfalls:

- **Product adoption is not a customer problem.** Customers don't care if "metrics are declining" or "people aren't using the product." Frame the problem from the customer perspective.
- **Start with the end customer's problem.** Even if you build

products for other internal teams or partners, start with your
end customer's problem.
- **Writing the problem down doesn't mean that you're done.**
  You need to do the work to understand if this is a real
  problem that many of your customers share.

This first step is just a hypothesis. You can't answer this question
without working on the next one.

How Do We Know That This Problem Exists?

Understanding if the customer problem exists is hard work. This
work could include:

- Talking to at least five customers about the problem.
- Diving into existing metrics and research about the problem.
- Discussing the problem with experts in your organization
  (e.g. user research, support).
- Running a simple A/B test to validate if the problem exists.
- Researching competitors to understand how they're tackling
  the problem.

During this process, you may find that what you think is a problem
doesn't actually exist. Or, you may find that customers have a bigger
pain point that you should solve instead. This is great because your
goal is not just to solve any problem; it's to solve your customer's most
important problem. Usually, this is a problem that many people
share, but that doesn't mean that it will be easy to identify. If you
work on a mobile app, for example, you could get complaints from
power users about receiving too many push notifications. But is that
the right problem to prioritize, or do most users receive no notifications at all?

Too many people write what they think is a customer problem and jump directly to finding a solution for it. Don't make that mistake. Take the time to validate that your customer problem actually exists.

Why Is It Critical That We Solve This Problem?

Now that you understand the customer problem, shift your attention toward your company. How will solving this problem help your company achieve its mission and grow its metrics? We'll discuss this step in the next chapter.

11

SELECTING A GOAL METRIC

Selecting a goal metric to focus on is hard. Well-chosen metrics motivate your team to ship great products. Poorly chosen metrics can lead to wrong trade-offs that hurt your product, company, and customers. To identify the right goal metric, you need to answer three questions:

1. Is growing the metric good for customers and the company?
2. Is the metric easy to understand and measure?
3. Can my team directly grow this metric?

Is Growing the Metric Good for Customers and the Company?

Being metrics obsessed is not the same as being customer obsessed.

A common pitfall is when the goals of your team and your company are not aligned. For example, a feed team for a video site could set interactions (comments, likes, etc.) as their goal metric. This goal could lead to product decisions like always showing expanded comments in feed. But that could easily hurt the overall company metric of minutes watched because the videos themselves will have less visibility.

An even worse pitfall is when the goals of your team and your customers are not aligned. For example, suppose you were in charge of user profiles for a social network. You set a goal to grow profile completeness—that is, the percent of user profiles that have their information filled out (e.g., education, job history). The easiest way to achieve your goal is to ask users questions like: "What job do you have?" "Where did you grow up?" Your completeness metric skyrockets, and you've given the social network more data for advertisers to target. But how do your users feel about always being asked for their personal information?

Is the Metric Easy to Understand and Measure?

Can you explain this metric to your CEO in less than 30 seconds? If the metric starts declining, can you break it down to figure out why?

A common pitfall is selecting an overly complicated metric. For example, suppose you're in charge of growing drivers for Uber. You have data showing that 20% of drivers (let's call them full-time drivers) are responsible for 80% of rides. You see that only 10% of part-time drivers are converting to full time, so you set a goal to double part-time to full-time conversion to 20%. But is a 20% conversion rate good or bad? What happens if you convert riders to full-time drivers, but those riders were never part-time drivers? You could have saved yourself many headaches by setting a simple goal to grow the number of full-time drivers.

Can My Team Directly Grow This Metric?

Is this metric directly under your team's control? If you run an experiment, can you show statistically significant results quickly? Is your team excited about growing this metric?

A common pitfall is selecting a metric that your team can't move directly (talk about demoralizing them!). For example, if you're a video product manager, growing video views could be your goal. But if 90% of your product's views are coming from feed and the feed team is not aligned, you will have a hard time reaching the goal. Can you find other discovery channels? Or can you convince the feed team that giving videos better discovery also helps their goal metric?

To avoid this pitfall, classify the metrics that you track as outputs and inputs. Outputs are goal metrics that you'll use to measure success. Inputs are metrics that your team has direct control over that also grow your outputs.

For example, let's assume that you're the product manager in charge of sending emails reminding Netflix subscribers to renew their subscriptions. Your output might be retention rate (percent of subscribers who renew each month). Your inputs could include email sends, opens, and clicks on a "renew subscription" button from your e-mail. If you can't brainstorm clear inputs for your output or if your inputs rely too much on other teams, chances are your team won't be able to grow your output directly.

Finding a Great Metric to Grow Is a Collaborative Process

You must get your team, your management chain, and any adjacent teams to internalize why you selected this metric for it to be effective. Make sure you have a clear problem statement before trying to pick a metric to grow. Then, walk through the above questions with your team to validate whether the metric is a good fit.

Once you understand the customer problem and your goal metric, you can move on to the "identify" phase of the loop. Start by making sure that your team has a great mission, vision, and strategy.

12

MISSION, VISION, AND STRATEGY

You can't define a great product if your team doesn't have an overall mission, vision, and strategy:

- **Mission** is why your team exists. It's the big, audacious goal that inspires your team to succeed.
- **Vision** is what the world will look like once you make significant progress toward your mission.
- **Strategy** is how your team will achieve your mission and vision.

Understand the 3Cs First: Customer, Company, and Competition

You need to dive into the "understand" phase of the product development loop before you can define a mission, vision, and strategy. Having a clear sense of your customer's needs, your company's goals, and your competition's products (in that priority order) is a prerequisite.

If you're new to a team, spend a month or two just developing this understanding. Unlike roadmaps and individual product requirements, your mission, vision, and strategy should rarely change. So take the time to gather feedback from all stakeholders and get the "understand" phase right before you proceed.

What Makes a Great Mission, Vision, and Strategy?

A simple way to measure the effectiveness of your mission, vision, and strategy is to ask three people on your team to say it back to you. If they all say the same thing, you're probably on the right track.

Does this mean that you should repeat your mission, vision, and strategy all the time? Yes, but that's only half the story. The other half is that you should craft statements that make sense and are memorable by themselves. People on your team should feel excited about these statements because they remind them why they come to work every day and empower them to make better decisions.

Let's evaluate Amazon's mission, vision, and strategy as an example:

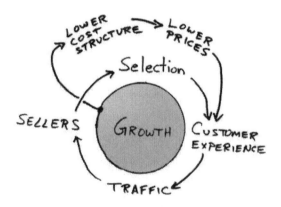

Figure 3. *Amazon's strategy flywheel.*

Mission: To be Earth's most customer centric company.

Vision: To build a place where people can come to find anything they might want to buy online.

Strategy: To offer the lowest prices, the widest selection, and the best customer experience.

AMAZON SERVES a wide variety of customers (e.g., consumers, sellers, creators, developers) in hundreds of different businesses. Yet its mission, vision, and strategy help Amazon employees make better decisions every day. A mission to be the Earth's most customer-centric company means that every employee must work backward from the customer problem and promptly address customer complaints. A vision to help people find anything they want online pushes Amazon to expand to new verticals like apparel and pharmacy. Finally, a strategy to offer the widest selection at the lowest prices with the best customer experience applies to every Amazon team—from online video to Amazon Web Services.

Let's dive into how you can craft a great mission, vision, and strategy.

Mission and Vision

A great mission and vision has three traits:

1. It solves a real **customer problem.**
2. It **inspires** your team.
3. It helps people **make decisions.**

Consider the Kindle team's mission and vision statement: "To make available in less than 60 seconds every book ever written, in any language, in print or out of print."[1] It's clear that this statement solves a real customer problem and is inspirational, but let's imagine how it can help the Kindle team make decisions. Suppose that the team is trying to decide whether authors should be able to publish to Kindle directly, which could hurt Kindle's established publisher partnerships. But if the mission and vision is to make available every book ever written (instead of just books from established authors), then the decision should be to give every author a chance to reach an audience, even if they don't have a traditional publisher.

The Kindle team has one statement for both their mission (long-term goal) and vision (what success looks like), and that's OK. The fewer words your team has to remember, the more likely they are to keep the mission and vision top of mind.

Strategy

In his book *Good Strategy/Bad Strategy*, Richard Rumelt wrote:[2]

> At the core, strategy is about focus, and most complex organizations don't focus their resources. Instead, they pursue multiple goals at once, not concentrating enough resources to achieve a breakthrough in any of them.

According to Rumelt, a great strategy has three components:

- A **diagnosis** of the major challenges that are preventing you from achieving your mission.
- An **overarching plan** to overcome those challenges.
- A **set of actions** to accomplish the plan.

I think one of the best examples of a great strategy is Elon Musk's first master plan for Tesla. In 2006, Tesla's mission was to accelerate the world's transition to sustainable transport. Its vision was to create the most compelling car company of the 21st century by driving the world's transition to electric vehicles. But Elon's masterstroke was in laying out Tesla's strategy:[3]

> Diagnosis: In 2006, Tesla only had enough money to make a low volume, expensive car.

> Strategy: Elon planned to "enter at the high end of the market, where customers are prepared to pay a premium and then drive

down market as fast as possible to higher unit volume and lower prices with each successive model."

Set of actions: To achieve his plan, Tesla first built the Roadster, a low volume, expensive sports car. It then used those earnings to develop medium volume cars (Model S and X) before finally shipping an affordable, mass market car (Model 3).

The strategy didn't work out precisely as Elon wanted. For example, the Model S cost almost as much as the Roadster instead of "half the Roadster's price point" and the Model 3 took longer to build at scale than expected. But Tesla's master plan had all the elements of good strategy (diagnosis, overarching plan, set of actions) and empowered Tesla employees to focus on executing toward a shared mission.

Before we close this chapter, let's examine a company that didn't have a great strategy. In 2011, Evernote had a great mission and vision to help people remember everything. Its major challenges were a buggy core app and new competitors like Google Docs that allowed people to collaborate on documents together. Instead of creating a plan to address these challenges, Evernote launched new apps (e.g., Evernote Food helped people log meals) and physical notebooks. When this strategy failed, the company went through multiple CEO changes and is still trying to recover today.

To summarize, a great mission, vision, and strategy gives people on your team a shared purpose (why), a picture of what success looks like (what), and a plan to make that vision a reality (how).

13

BUILDING A PRODUCT ROADMAP

Once you've aligned on a mission, vision, and strategy with your team, the next step is to break your strategy down into an actionable roadmap. The roadmap should give people a clear sense of your team's objectives and key results for a specific period. It should also describe the features that your team will build to achieve those results.

Objectives and Key Results (OKRs)

Andy Grove created the objective and key results framework when he was Intel's CEO in the 1980s. According to Andy, an objective is a qualitative goal that your team wants to achieve, and key results are quantitative measures of progress toward the objective.

OKRs serve three purposes in roadmap planning. First, they allow your team to execute by breaking down your strategy into actionable goals and milestones. Second, they empower teams to work effectively together by aligning on shared OKRs upfront. Finally, management uses OKRs to measure your team's performance.

Despite these benefits, OKRs are meant to be a guide, not a binding contract. Although it shouldn't happen often, you should have the flexibility to change your team's OKRs if you have a solid reason to do so. As Andy describes:[1]

> If the supervisor manually relies on OKRs to evaluate his subordinate's performance, or if the subordinate uses it rigidly and forgoes taking advantage of an opportunity because it was not a specific OKR, then both are behaving in a petty and unprofessional fashion.

To illustrate this point, let's use Christopher Columbus's discovery of the Americas as an example. In 1492, Queen Isabella of Spain had an objective to increase the country's wealth. To achieve her objective, she sponsored Columbus, her subordinate, to find a new trade route to Asia. Columbus measured progress through several key results, from acquiring ships to restocking supplies in the Canary Islands before his long journey. Instead of reaching Asia, Columbus discovered the Americas, which brought significant wealth to Spain. If Queen Isabella only evaluated Columbus based on his original OKRs, he would've failed.

So use common sense when setting OKRs and measuring your team's progress.

How Can OKRs Be Used to Structure Your Roadmap?

In the previous chapter, we covered how you can craft a compelling mission, vision, and strategy with your team. A roadmap uses OKRs to outline how your team will execute on your strategy in the next three to twelve months.

Start the roadmap with an overview of your team's mission, vision, and strategy. Follow that with a list of OKRs and the features that your team will build to achieve each key result in the upcoming quarter.

————

To understand this structure better, let's walk through a sample quarterly roadmap for the Instagram growth team:

1. Overview

The opening paragraph of your roadmap should highlight your team's mission, vision, and strategy before summarizing what your goal metric is for the quarter.

> The mission of the Instagram growth team is to help people find meaningful communities based on what matters most to them. Our strategy is to bring new people to Instagram and connect them to accounts and communities that interest them. In Q4 2019, we want to grow the global Instagram community from 1B to 1.05B members (+5%) through the following objectives and key results.

2. Objectives

Objectives are qualitative goals that your team will focus on in the quarter. Objectives come from your strategy, and since good strategy is about focus, your roadmap should ideally have only three objectives per quarter:

> Acquisition – Bring new people to Instagram.
>
> Activation – Build a fast, seamless sign-up experience.
>
> Connection – Help new Instagram users form meaningful connections.

3. Key Results

Each objective should have one or more KRs (key results). As you write each KR, briefly describe why the KR matters, who the owners are, and what dependencies it has.

Objective: Activation – Build a fast, seamless sign-up experience.

KR: Improve mobile web sign up rate by 5%.

We want to focus on mobile web this quarter because it is by far our largest acquisition channel (60% of total) yet has the worst sign up rates (30%).

Owners: Pat (product manager), Susan (design), Dave (eng).

Dependencies: Infra team to improve mobile web page latency.

4. Features

Below each KR, describe at a high level the features you plan to build to achieve it. Wherever possible, include a ship date for each feature, even if that date is just a rough month estimate.

Objective: Activation – Build a fast, seamless sign-up experience.

KR: Improve mobile web sign up rate by 5%.

We want to focus on mobile web this quarter because it is by far our largest acquisition channel (60% of total) yet has the worst sign up rates (30%).

Owners: Pat (product manager), Susan (design), Dave (eng).

Dependencies: Infra team to improve mobile web page latency.

Features:

1. Reduce the number of mobile web sign up steps from 5 to 2 (January).

2. Ship username suggestions (March).

How Does Roadmap Prioritization Work?

So how do you actually decide which objectives and features to prioritize in your roadmap? Prioritization is more art than science, but let's walk through two frameworks that you can use.

Prioritize Objectives

Start by prioritizing objectives, not individual features. It's useful to think about prioritizing objectives as a Venn diagram with three lenses: customer, business, and vision. The customer lens wants you to address your customer's most burning problems. The business lens wants you to grow your team and your company's goal metrics. Finally, the vision lens wants you to get one step closer to making your long-term vision a reality.

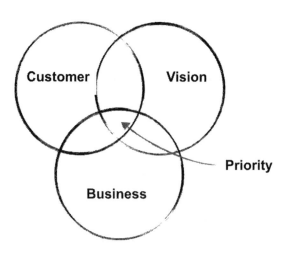

Figure 4. *Use the customer, vision, and business lenses to prioritize objectives in your roadmap.*

Prioritize objectives at the intersection of all three lenses. If that's not possible, then you should try to balance your objectives across the three lenses. For example, if you only prioritize what customers ask for, you'll never work on monetization objectives, since customers prefer free products. If you only prioritize growing your goal metric, you may only build short-term hacks and lose sight of your long-term vision.

Prioritize Features Under Each OKR

Finding balance is also important when prioritizing individual features under each objective. Think of prioritizing features as mapping them to two axes on a chart: value and effort.

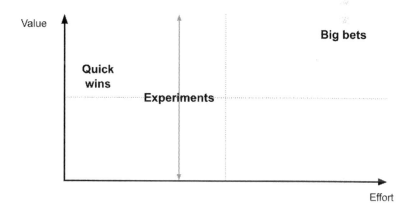

Figure 5. *Find balance between quick wins, experiments, and big bets when prioritizing features in your roadmap.*

To determine value, use the three lenses to understand the benefit that your feature will deliver to customers, your company, and your vision. To determine effort, work with your engineers to cost estimate each feature (e.g., low, medium, high). Once you map all the features that your team can build to these two axes, you'll see three types of features emerge:

- **Quick wins** (medium-high value, low effort) are usually no-brainers to build. However, if you only build quick wins, you may never make a big bet that could transform how customers use your product.

- **Big bets** (high value, high effort) are features that you're confident will deliver significant value to your customer and company. However, big bets are expensive, so you shouldn't commit to more than one or two per quarter.
- **Experiments** (? value, low effort) are features that could deliver a lot of value or none. It's worth shipping a few of these quickly before deciding whether to invest further.

In any quarter, I recommend that you find the right balance between one or two big bets and a few quick wins and experiments.

Tips for Building Product Roadmaps

Here are a few more tips for building product roadmaps and setting OKRs:

1. **Start the process early.** At least a month before a new quarter begins, start brainstorming OKRs with your team. Once you have an initial list of OKRs, meet with other teams to identify dependencies and start sharing your roadmap with your management chain.

2. **Aim to achieve at least 70% of your OKRs.** If your team is consistently hitting all their OKRs, you're not ambitious enough. If your team is missing most of their OKRs, they'll likely lose motivation. A 70% goal encourages your team to stretch their capabilities without risking too much failure.

3. **Set OKRs based on the team you're on.** If you're on a platform team, your roadmap will be less flexible as internal teams will depend on your team's work. As a result, you may set OKRs for shipping individual platform updates. If you're on a growth team, your OKRs should focus on metrics. For example, you might set a KR to grow sign-up rates by 5%,

while keeping the flexibility to change what features you
build based on your learnings throughout the quarter.

To set effective OKRs, your team will need to know, at a high level,
what products they'll build in the quarter. They'll need product
requirements to estimate the time it'll take to ship the product. We'll
cover defining individual products next.

14

DEFINING PRODUCT REQUIREMENTS

The product requirements document (PRD) captures the problem, goal metric, and solution all in one place. Unlike roadmaps, PRDs are focused on a single product.

In this chapter, we'll start by walking through a typical PRD. We'll then walk through what Amazon calls a press release / FAQ, which I recommend that you write in addition to a PRD for major new product initiatives.

————

Product Requirement Document

PRDs come in various templates. I like to include six main sections:

1. Header
2. Problem
3. Goal
4. Requirements
5. Design

6. FAQ

Let's walk through a hypothetical PRD for a simple experiment at Pinterest. If you're not familiar with Pinterest, it's a visual discovery platform for interests and ideas.

1. Header

Start the PRD by listing the key stakeholders involved in the project along with links to other related documents.

> **Experiment: Topic selector during new user onboarding**
>
> Pinterest | January 2020 | Joe Smith
>
> <u>Stakeholders</u>
>
> Product - Joe Smith
>
> Design - Anna Taylor
>
> Engineering - Ben Gordon
>
> Marketing - Kate Wong
>
> Analytics - Jeff Levine
>
> <u>Link to Design, Engineering Epic</u>

2. Problem

Summarize the customer problem by answering these questions in one or two paragraphs:

- What is the customer problem?
- How do we know that this is a problem?
- Why is it critical that we solve this problem?

<u>Problem</u>

People want to view and pin content for topics they're interested in. Today, everyone who signs up for Pinterest sees the same feed of the most popular content. Categories like women's fashion and decor dominate this feed. We believe that allowing people to select topics during onboarding to personalize their feed will increase activation rates and help Pinterest grow.

3. Hypothesis

Summarize your goal metric and what success looks like in a single sentence:

We can grow (goal metric) by (amount) if we (build this feature).

Hypothesis

We can grow activation rate by adding a "Pick topics to personalize your feed" screen to the new user onboarding flow.

4. Metrics

List all the metrics that you want to track to understand how your product is doing. You should split this list into output metrics (which you will use to measure success) and input metrics (which are levers that you can pull to grow your output).

Outputs – Activation rate (% of new sign-ups who visit again in 7 days)

Inputs

Number of users who:

- Visit topic selector screen

- Select a topic

- Click done button

- Pin during their first session

5. Requirements

This is where you should define exactly what the product is. Write product requirements as user stories:

As a (user type), when I (perform an action), then (this happens).

The above format makes it easy for people reading the requirements to understand what your product is from the customer's perspective and for an engineer to copy and paste your stories into engineering tickets.

As a user, when I am signing up to Pinterest, then I see a "Pick 5 or more topics to personalize your feed" screen.

On this screen, I see a grid of topics and a button at the bottom.

When I tap a topic (e.g. Food and Drink), then I see a check mark showing that I selected the topic.

When I have selected less than 5 topics, then the button is grayed out and displays text "Pick x more" (with X being 5 subtracted by the number of topics I've selected so far).

When I have selected 5 or more topics, then the button is active and displays text "Done"

When I click the "Done" button, then I visit my Pinterest home feed that's personalized based on the topics I've selected.

6. Design

The design gives people an immediate understanding of the user experience. You should get your designer involved as early as possible because he or she will often have great ideas on what the product requirements should be. If your designer is busy, create a hand-drawn visual or wireframe yourself.

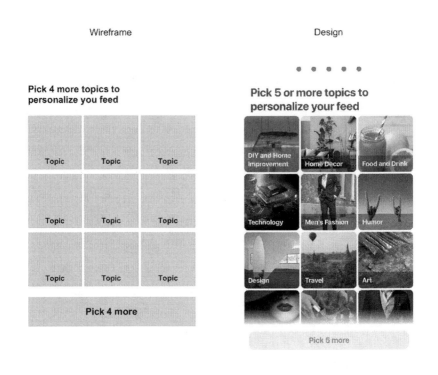

Figure 6. *Your design can start as a simple wireframe before eventually becoming a high-fidelity mock-up.*

7. Launch Plan

If you're launching an experiment, describe which users are eligible, what the test and control groups are, and what the ramp plan is.

Eligibility: People who sign up for Pinterest on web and mobile web.

Test: Experience described above.

Control: Existing onboarding experience without "topic selector" screen.

Ramp plan: 50% test and 50% control.

If you're launching a larger feature that requires press and marketing, your launch plan will be more complex. We'll cover a sample launch checklist in the Project Management chapter.

———

Press Release / FAQs

The press release is an internal document that all Amazon product managers write for major new product initiatives. I love the press release because it is the embodiment of working backwards from the customer problem.

When you're writing a press release, imagine that it's the first thing customers read to understand how your product solves their problem. Think of your customers—not internal stakeholders—as the target audience for this document.

Let's walk through a hypothetical press release using our problem statement example from the Customer Problem chapter:

Problem: Today, working professionals don't have the time or mental energy to shop for groceries and prepare healthy meals.

To define a product that addresses this problem, we'll write a simplified press release for Amazon Go, the company's grocery store chain that features no lines and no checkouts.[1]

1. Header

Start your press release with a header that describes what you're launching and why customers should care. Add a date to set expectations on when you expect the product to launch.

Introducing Amazon Go, a grocery store with no lines or checkouts

January, 2018 – Get the food you love, then get going with
Amazon Go.

2. Describe the Problem

The opening paragraph of your press release should focus on the
customer problem and the most critical customer benefit that you're
delivering. Your goal is to leave customers excited to read more.

> Many working professionals don't have the time or mental energy to
> shop for groceries and prepare healthy meals. Today, they have to
> visit their local grocery store after work, wait in line at checkout, and
> then go home to cook. With Amazon Go, they can walk into a store,
> grab what they want (including ready-made meals), and just
> walk out.

3. Customer Quote

A customer quote is a powerful way of describing why customers
should care about your product using their language. You can make
this up, or even better, get a direct customer quote during beta testing. To create a great quote, imagine how you want the customer to
feel and how they would express their delight about your product.

> "I went to my local Amazon Go store today." said Jane, a working
> mom with two kids at home. "I grabbed a few of their pre-made
> salads and was in and out in less than five minutes. Not having to
> wait in line at checkout is a game-changer!"

4. Describe the Solution

Your press release should describe your product experience in simple
terms, so customers understand how to find and use your product.

Here's how Amazon Go works: First, scan the Amazon Go app to enter the store. Then, put away your phone and start shopping. Take whatever you like, and we'll automatically add each item to your in-app shopping cart. Once you have everything you want, you can just walk out, and we'll send you a receipt through your Amazon account.

5. Call to Action

Close the press release with a call to action on how customers can start using your product now.

Amazon Go is available in Seattle, Chicago, San Francisco, and New York City, with more locations coming soon. Visit amazon.com/go to find a store near you.

6. FAQs

After your press release, list frequently asked questions about your product to help keep your team aligned and to unpack assumptions. A FAQ for Amazon Go can include questions such as:

What is Amazon Go?

How does Amazon Go work?

What can I buy at Amazon Go?

Do you have people working in the store?

———

Tips for Writing PRDs and Press Release / FAQs

Here are a few more tips for writing these documents:

1. **Keep it short.** Try to keep your PRDs and press release / FAQs to 2-4 pages.
2. **Don't bury the lede.** Open your PRD or press release with the customer problem and the most important benefit that you're delivering to the customer.
3. **Review, review, review.** Keep working on these documents until each paragraph flows. If your document doesn't feel great after multiple iterations, that's a signal that your product may not be worth building.
4. **Sometimes a press release isn't necessary.** If you're building a small feature, you don't need to write a press release. Instead, you can summarize the problem and the most important benefit in a few paragraphs at the beginning of the PRD.

15

GREAT PROJECT MANAGEMENT

You've defined a great product, and everyone is excited to build it. Now it's time to start the third phase of product development: execution.

To execute, you need to help your team navigate through the following stages:

Figure 7. *The execution phase of product development.*

1. Kick-Off

During the kick off stage, your goal is to help your team build a shared understanding of the PRD and the project's key milestones:

- **Review the PRD.** Hold a kickoff meeting and walk your team through the customer problem, goal, and product requirements. Leave time to answer questions.
- **Set clear milestones.** Work with your engineering manager to break the product requirements into tickets and ask your engineers to estimate how long each ticket will take. Group tickets into milestones with clear dates and exit criteria. For example, a milestone could be completing the backend service before tackling the user interface. Two milestones that every project should have are dogfood and launch.
- **Create one channel for communication.** After the kickoff meeting, create a project channel and invite all stakeholders to it. Pin the PRD, milestones, designs, tickets, and any other relevant materials to the channel. You're now ready to build the product!

2. Kick-Off → Dogfood

During the kick-off → dogfood stage,[1] your goal is to help your team stay focused on shipping. To do this, you need to:

- **Communicate constantly.** Set up weekly team meetings to review progress and identify blockers. Post notes from every meeting in your project channel so that everyone is on the same page.
- **Manage dependencies.** Hopefully, you've already established shared OKRs with teams upon which your project has dependencies. Even with shared OKRs, teams can still fall behind on their work, and miscommunications can happen. That's why it's essential to communicate regularly, especially when two teams are working together for the first time.
- **Address risks and blockers.** During development, unexpected blockers or risks can surface. Perhaps an engineer will ask you to cut scope because a ticket is taking

much longer to complete than expected. Or maybe you've uncovered new user research that requires additional product changes. We'll discuss this more in the Making Good Decisions chapter.

3. Dogfood → Launch

During the dogfood → launch stage, your goal is to help your team squash bugs and get ready for launch.

- **Test rigorously.** Be alert and pay attention to the details to avoid delays close to launch. Test the product rigorously yourself to set the example for your team. When you reach dogfood, send an e-mail asking people in your organization to test the product and create a feedback channel for them to report bugs. Invite everyone in the feedback channel to bug bashes. A constant stream of feedback is the lifeblood of high-quality products.
- **Build a launch checklist.** A simple checklist will help ensure that everyone knows what they need to do to get ready for launch. Review your list regularly with your team to stay on track.

Task	Owner	Due	Status
Before launch			
Bug bash	Joe, EM	7/10/2019	Done
Confirm all data logging is working	Sean, analytics	7/15/2019	
Legal review	Dawn, legal	7/20/2019	
Draft blog post staged	Diane, marketing	7/25/2019	
Day of launch (8/5/2019)			
Push to prod	David, eng	10 AM	
Ramp to 5%	David, eng	10 AM	
Ramp to 100%	David, eng	12 PM	
Publish blog post		12 PM	

Figure 8. *An example launch checklist that includes a list of tasks, owners, dates, and current status.*

4. Launch → Retro

During the launch → retro stage, your goal is to celebrate shipping with your team while paying attention to customer feedback and metrics.

- **Celebrate the launch.** Launch day is a time for celebration. Email your organization to let people know that the product has shipped and publicly thank everyone who contributed.
- **Monitor post launch activity.** As the product owner, it's your job to keep a close eye on how your product is doing. Look for early feedback from customers and metrics. By monitoring post-launch activity and quickly fixing issues that come up, you can accelerate growth for a product that otherwise would have faltered. Remember that your success is measured by whether you solved the customer problem and grew your goal metric, not by shipping the product.
- **Hold a team retro.** Discuss with your team what went well, what went wrong, and what the learnings were while working on the project. The more lessons you can identify and internalize as a team, the better your team will become at navigating the "understand, identify, and execute" loop.

Now that we covered each stage of the execution phase, let's dive into several essential skills that you need to navigate the product development loop.

16

EFFECTIVE COMMUNICATION

Effective communication is essential for product managers. It's nearly impossible to over-communicate, so let's dive into the two major channels of communication: writing and meetings.

———

Writing

Writing full sentences forces you to think through your arguments and present them in a structured way. Writing also gives every reader in your company the opportunity to understand what you're trying to communicate without you having to be there to explain it to them.

The secret to writing well is to keep it simple, short, and specific.

Simple: Get to the Point

When you're writing, your primary goal is to communicate a single point. Here's how you can structure your document to keep it simple:

1. Start with the main point.
2. Follow up with no more than three supporting arguments.

Start with the main point because your readers are busy. If the first paragraph doesn't tell them what they need to know, they will not read the rest of your document. By stating the main point up front, you're showing your readers you're confident about your argument. Those who have questions can easily read more to understand your supporting arguments.

Follow up with no more than three supporting arguments because most readers don't like to remember more than three things. If they have to read through a laundry list of arguments, they will tune out. Worse, you've shown readers you don't know which arguments are the most important.

Think of someone reading your document as peeling an onion. The more your readers have to dig to understand what you're trying to communicate—peel the onion—the more annoyed they'll get. Most people will not keep peeling the onion, so make sure you get to the point right away.

Short: Aim for Two Pages

In *The Elements of Style,* Strunk & White wrote about why it's important to keep your writing concise:[1]

> Vigorous writing is concise. A sentence should contain no unnecessary words, a paragraph no unnecessary sentences, for the same reason that a drawing should contain no unnecessary lines and a machine no unnecessary parts. This requires not that the writer make all his sentences short, or that he avoid all detail and treat his subjects only in outline, but that every word tell.

One of the best ways to keep your writing simple is to keep it short. Every word that you add lessens the impact of all the other words.

Amazon forces all product managers to write documents that are no more than six pages. However, I've found that most of the time you can make your argument in just one to two pages. If you have to, you can include more details in an appendix or FAQ.

Specific: Remove Uncertainty

Don't make your readers guess what you're trying to communicate. Here's an example:

> *Our product's user base grew a lot over the past month.*

This statement raises many questions: "How many users were added?" "From when to when did this happen?" Here's a much better sentence:

> *From 4/1 to 4/30, our product grew from 100 to 120 daily active users (+20%).*

Be as specific as possible in your communication to remove uncertainty.

Tips for Writing Well

Here are a few more tips that will help keep your writing simple, short, and specific:

Writing Process

1. **Write for your audience.** Think about who's most likely to read your document and put yourself in that person's shoes. Try to understand what that person cares about and what they already know. For example, an executive is less likely to be interested in implementation details compared to an engineer on your team.

2. **Review and edit all the time.** Review and edit your document to fix grammar and streamline paragraphs to simplify your writing. Read a printout of your document or say the words out loud to get a sense of how it flows from a different perspective.

3. **Ask knowledgeable people to review.** Preview your document with knowledgeable people so they can provide feedback. Ask someone who's not familiar with your project to read your document to see if they can understand your main points.

4. **Answer the most common questions.** As you and others review the document, make a note of the most common questions that come up. Revise your document to answer these questions, either in the narrative or in the FAQ.

Writing Style

1. **Make your writing scannable.** Your headings and formatting should allow your readers to quickly scan your document to understand your main arguments.

2. **Use the active voice.** The active voice is more direct and confident than the passive one. For example, write "We will grow users by..." instead of "A series of improvements will help us grow users."

3. **Don't use complicated words.** Try to avoid using complex words, jargon, or acronyms as much as possible. If you must use an acronym, explain what it means the first time that you use it.

4. **Remove words that introduce uncertainty.** Avoid words like should, might, could, probably, and maybe in your writing. Replace these words with data or a statement of fact.

5. **Only include charts if you can defend all the numbers.** If you add a chart, people will look at all the numbers on it and ask questions. Often, it's easier to show only the numbers that matter in a sentence or table.

_____

Meetings

Sometimes even the best written communication isn't enough to get people aligned, so you must schedule a meeting. Many product managers spend their days in meetings. Others try to block off time on their calendars to avoid meetings and focus on work.

These tactics seem to suggest that meetings are a waste of time. In reality, an efficient meeting is one of the best ways to make decisions and reach alignment. Let's dive into four types of meetings and how you can run them efficiently:

- 1:1s
- Team meetings
- Ad hoc meetings
- Product review

1:1

The 1:1 is the best meeting to be radically transparent.

Use the 1:1 to care personally about your coworker by asking what's on her mind and showing appreciation. Ask her for candid feedback about how you can improve and offer the same feedback in return if you think it'll help her performance. Finally, empower her by making sure that you're both aligned on the goal of your project and asking "what can I do to help?"

You should schedule recurring 1:1s with your manager, skip-level manager, your peers (e.g., designer, engineering manager), and your reports. Even if you see them every day, nothing beats a private half-hour conversation where you can be open about real issues.

Team Meeting

The team meeting is a weekly sync with people who are working on your project. These meetings should have both a fixed agenda and time for open discussion. The fixed agenda part usually involves reviewing the metrics, tracking the project's status, or diving deep on a specific topic. The open discussion part (5-10 minutes in the end) allows people to bring up issues or concerns about the project.

If you're running this meeting, it's your job to keep the agenda on track and encourage people to participate. The structure of this meeting should be so clear and repetitive that anyone on your team can run it if you're not there.

Ad Hoc Meeting

Ad hoc meetings are for making decisions that you didn't have time to make in your team meeting. No one likes to have ad hoc meetings pop up in their calendar, so it's especially important to run these meetings efficiently. Before you call an ad hoc meeting, you need to clearly understand what decision you're trying to make and who should be part of the decision-making process.

Product Review

The product review is a meeting where you present your roadmap to executives. Product reviews don't happen often but give product managers a lot of stress because they want to show executives they know what they're talking about.

The goal of the product review is not to provide a status update, but to get executive input on a key decision that you're trying to make. Executives have limited time and bandwidth to think about your problem but can provide valuable insight into how it fits with the company's overall strategy.

That's why you need to share the problem and decision that you're trying to make upfront before presenting supporting evidence. Product reviews are successful if you can get aligned with executives on what you're trying to build or if an executive can help you unblock a decision. For example, two teams may have different goals and need executive input to align on a path forward.

Tips for Running Meetings

Here are a few more tips to make your meetings more productive:

1. **Focus on the why first.** What is the goal of the meeting? What problem are people in the room trying to solve?
2. **Have a mindset of "how can I help you."** Walk into each meeting with a mindset of "How can I help you." Don't be afraid to ask directly: "How can I help you make this project more successful?"
3. **Have an agenda.** During the meeting, make sure that the agenda is visible so that everyone knows what will be covered. List your agenda items on a slide or the whiteboard. Highlight the issue you're talking about and cross out the items above it so that everyone knows what the current topic is. Using numbered lists makes it easy for people to refer back to things (e.g., "So going back to #1...") and for people who are late to the meeting to understand where the discussion is.
4. **Keep meetings focused.** If someone is talking about something that's not related to the goal or is meant to be covered later, please interrupt them. Remind them of the purpose of the meeting and request that they discuss it another time. You may think this is rude, but other people will appreciate that you are keeping the meeting focused.
5. **Send notes right after the meeting.** A meeting where people made decisions that were not documented never happened. Make sure you send out notes right after the

meeting or at least on the same day. These notes don't have to be super polished and just need to cover the main points. Your goal is to document the key decisions so that everyone can refer back to them. I've found sending notes one of the best ways for new product managers to show value because most people can't be bothered to do it.

Besides excellent communication, you also need to be effective at making decisions. We'll cover that in the next chapter.

17

MAKING GOOD DECISIONS

As a product manager, you need to make decisions about your product every day. Unfortunately, you're almost never going to have all the information that you need to decide. Making good decisions despite uncertainty is a critical skill for PMs.

So how do you make good decisions? Think of your decision making as optimizing for two axes:

1. Was it the right decision?
2. Did you decide fast enough?

If you always wait to make the right decision, you could delay the project by making your team wait too long for the next steps. But if you always make decisions quickly without evaluating the facts, you could waste your team's time by making the wrong decisions constantly.

One-Way and Two-Way Doors

When thinking about whether to optimize for decision quality or speed, it's valuable to think of decisions as one-way or two-way doors. Two-way doors are decisions that can be easily reversed if you're wrong, so prioritize decision speed. One-way doors are rarer. These decisions cannot be reversed easily, so try to gather more information if you're uncertain.

If you're struggling to make a decision that's a one-way door, seek knowledgeable people who disagree. Discussing the decision with experts who you trust (including your customer, if possible) will help you get closer to the truth. Don't delay the decision forever, however. Even for one-way doors, try to decide when you have about 70% of the information.

Don't Compromise If You Think You're Right, Find the Truth

When you're trying to make a decision with a group of people, it's natural to want to compromise to avoid damaging your relationship with others. This desire is especially true if the decision-maker is your manager or an executive. But if you genuinely believe that the decision is wrong and have the evidence to back it up, you must have the courage to be the differing voice. Your goal is to find the truth no matter what, even when doing so is uncomfortable.

There's No Shame in Escalation

When two teams don't share the same goals, it becomes challenging to make a decision together. When you're stuck in these situations, escalate up the management chain. There's no shame in doing so because escalation is often more efficient than arguing back and forth over multiple meetings until both teams are exhausted.

Disagree and Commit

After people make a decision, you must commit yourself and your team to execute on it. Even if you don't agree with the decision, it's your job to make sure you understand why the decision was made and explain that to your team. It's never acceptable to say, "Because my boss said so."

Remember that decision making is a two-step process. When making a decision, you must find knowledgeable people to help you get closer to the truth. When a decision is made, you must focus on execution.

Tips for Making Good Decisions

Here are a few more tips for making good decisions:

1. **Express your opinion and encourage disagreement.** One way to listen is to state your opinion clearly and then going to great lengths to encourage disagreement.
2. **Data does not always equal truth.** Pay close attention when you or someone else is sharing data to support a decision. Ideally, there should be qualitative anecdotes to back up the data points.
3. **Ask questions to bring discussions back on track.** For conversations that are getting derailed, try asking: "How does this help the customer?" "What problem are we trying to solve?" and "What leads you to believe that's true?"
4. **Ask people to argue from the opposing perspective.** If two people passionately disagree about something, try asking them to argue from each other's perspective. If one of those people is you, the same tactic applies.
5. **Encourage people to participate.** If you think someone is not voicing their opinion, say "We're about to make a

decision that you argued against in the past but you have said nothing recently. Have you changed your mind?"

6. **Don't make decisions with too many people.** Ideally, there should be one clear decision maker and only eight people who are stakeholders in the decision. Smaller group debates are often better because they avoid groupthink.

18

INTERVIEW: SACHIN REKHI

Sachin is the CEO and co-founder of Notejoy, a collaborative notes platform for teams. Previously, he was a product lead at LinkedIn. In this interview, Sachin describes his journey to PM, his product planning process, and his advice for influencing people without authority.

Journey to Product Management

What made you want to be a product manager?

Early in my career, I worked at a telecom company called Paetec Communications as a software engineer. My job was to create an online billing tool that made it easy for the company's employees to process bills using PDFs.

I remember talking to an employee who used to have to print out bills manually to process them. With my tool, she could do all her work on the computer. She told me she almost cried when she found out that my software had saved her 18 hours of manual work each week.

This was my first experience delivering delight through software. I realized then that what I enjoyed was less about building the software itself but more about figuring out what to build in order to deliver delight. In other words, I realized that I wanted to be a product manager.

That's awesome. I think another interesting moment in your career was leaving LinkedIn to start your own company. What made you decide to do that?

Good question! At LinkedIn I was on track to become a general manager. We were working on Sales Navigator, which was a product for sales professionals, one of the main customer segments that LinkedIn serves.

I left because I felt that I was making incremental improvements to the product and I missed the day-to-day activity of talking to customers and crafting products based on their needs. I really wanted to go back to finding product-market fit for something new.

Specifically, I had experienced the pain and lack of delight in using existing collaboration tools to get a team of 500 people to work together on Sales Navigator. So, I saw collaboration software as an area of opportunity.

How does someone break into product if they have no product management experience?

There isn't really a degree you can get in product management and there isn't a single tried-and-true path. I think there are four common paths:

1. From college, the classic way is to get a computer science degree. That helps you better understand how technology works. Then look for an associate product manager role at a large company. These programs are great training for understanding the customer problem and working with other people to build delightful products.

2. If you're in a role where you work with product managers, you can try to transition to product in your current company. The key is to work closely with your PM to find time to work on more product-oriented projects. For example, as a marketer, you could try doing some inbound product research. Make it clear to your PM that you'd love to help on the product side and it's likely that he or she will value your thinking.

3. If you're a domain expert, you can leverage your knowledge to transition to product manager. I had a MD friend who joined a healthcare startup as a PM and another friend who had a masters of education that she leveraged to become a PM at an EdTech company.

4. Finally, if you're an entrepreneur, you're already exposed to many functions from engineering to sales to finance. Being able to wear multiple hats is a great skill set to have for a product manager.

Product Development at Notejoy

What's your vision for Notejoy?

Notejoy today is a collaborative notes app for any team. However, my vision for Notejoy is much broader.

I want Notejoy to be a product that helps unlock human potential by activating the world's collective wisdom. Let's break down what that means:

1. Unlock human potential: Notejoy is a tool that helps make humans more productive.

2. Collective wisdom: I think all of us have experienced how hard it is to ramp after joining a new company. It takes weeks and sometimes months to find out what's going on. Therefore, I think there's a lot of potential in activating the collective wisdom of teams and companies. I want Notejoy to

be a place where you can search for and find the collective wisdom of a company or a group of people.

Remember, in *The Matrix* when Neo plugged into the system and downloaded new knowledge in an instant? That's what I want Notejoy to be.

I love that movie and that's a big vision. What's your strategy to make it a reality?

Thank you! Yes, well, Notejoy today plays in multiple markets:

- <u>Notetaking app</u>: Like Apple Notes
- <u>Document collaboration</u>: Like Google Docs
- <u>One-stop shop to search for content</u>: Like Confluence and Wiki

I think our strategy is to deliver a minimum set of requirements across all three markets. We started with personal notetaking before expanding into document collaboration and we're just starting to tackle being a one-stop shop to search for content.

How do you decide what to build?

There's no formula to help me prioritize features, but I consider three different lenses:

The first lens is customer obsession. At Notejoy, I use a feedback tool that not only lets customers submit feedback but also lets them vote for features that they really want. This way, I'm keeping a constant pulse on what customers are asking for.

The second lens is the vision. Customers typically give tactical feedback but will not dream for you. I always keep Notejoy's vision— unlock human potential by activating the world's collective wisdom —in mind when I'm prioritizing features.

The final lens is business. At Notejoy, we need to continue to grow our business. This typically breaks down into acquisition, engagement, and monetization. I monitor metrics on each pillar and decide what metric we want to focus on improving next quarter.

There's a constant tension between all three lenses. For example, if I only listened to customers, I'll likely work on engagement features instead of monetization. And, product managers need to balance all three lenses to put together a product mix that makes sense.

What are some tools and processes that you use to help your team execute on the roadmap?

We make plans every year, every quarter, and every other week.

Every year, we do a post-mortem over what we accomplished in the previous year, whether that's growing a metric or building something that our customers have been asking for. The goal of this post-mortem is to understand what worked or didn't work. Using the insights from the post-mortem, I then put together a high-level annual plan for the year. At Notejoy, this annual planning process could take a few days but at a large company like LinkedIn, it could take a few weeks.

Every quarter, we produce a roadmap with OKRs (objective and key results). We usually have at least one OKR each for acquisition, engagement, and monetization that's tied to growing a metric. For example, acquisition might be new sign-ups, engagement might be 7-day retention, and monetization might be recurring revenue. I base these OKRs on our annual plan, which I also adjust based on what I learn each quarter.

Finally, every other week we do a sprint and try to ship something. Even at a start-up like Notejoy, I think having sprints gives us the rigor and cadence that we need to ensure that we're always shipping.

Since Notejoy is a collaboration tool, we use our own product to write our annual and quarterly plans.

Product Management Principles

How do you influence people without authority?

As a product manager, none of the people you need to build a great product report to you (e.g. executives, marketing, design), yet you're responsible for driving product results. Here are a three best practices that I follow to convince stakeholders:

1. **Explain the vision.** Always look for opportunities to share the goal that we're trying to solve for. Once people align to the goal, it becomes a lot easier to convince them to follow the tactics. For example, when walking through a feature in the roadmap, always explain why we're building it and how it helps our vision.

2. **Understand people's goals and try to find a win-win.** Make other people's problems your own. If you spend the time to deeply understand their goals upfront, they're much more likely to help you meet your goals.

3. **Invest in relationships.** I didn't appreciate this early in my career and I used to think company morale events were a waste of time. But now I realize how important it is to build genuine relationships with the people you work with. You need to understand where they're coming from and build rapport. It'll make resolving conflicts and driving results much easier.

How do you balance between presenting a compelling argument as a PM and being ready to admit when you're going the wrong direction with a product?

Product managers early in their career have a belief that they need to constantly defend their ideas. A better mentality is to be a truth seeker.

Truth seekers use every opportunity to find out what the truth is.

They listen carefully to other people's viewpoints instead of quickly trying to defend their own. They realize that listening to others will help them refine their ideas and get closer to the truth.

Truth seekers are a sponge for new ideas. I think new PMs are often fearful of having to manage too many ideas. But it's best to make people feel like you have truly heard them while helping them understand why you're not prioritizing their ideas right now. Sometimes you might be in the ninth inning of execution and you need to shut down an idea to execute and get something out there. That's ok, but use this hammer rarely.

19

INTERVIEW: LENNY RACHITSKY

Lenny is a former product lead of consumer supply growth at Airbnb. He writes a popular weekly e-mail newsletter that has a ton of useful information for product managers and founders.

How did you transition to product management?

I started my career in engineering before co-founding my start-up in Montreal, Canada. When Airbnb acquired it in 2012, I joined as an engineer. Over time, I found myself gravitating more and more to a product manager's responsibilities: running meetings, building roadmaps, and driving metrics.

Product management is often thankless, nerve-racking, and all-consuming but I can't imagine having another job. PMs are always closest to the center of the action and have a disproportionate amount of influence over key decisions.

Can you describe how roadmap planning at a company should work at a high level?

I like to use what I call the "W framework" to think about planning.

First, it's important to realize that there are two basic groups involved in building roadmaps:

- Leadership: Generally the executive staff of a company.
- Teams: The people executing the actual work.

Figure 9. *The W framework for roadmap planning.*

What role does each group play in the planning process?

The framework is shaped as a "W" because leadership and teams take turns in the planning process:

1. **Leadership provides context to the teams.** Leadership produces a high-level plan that includes the mission, vision, goals, and strategy of the company. The strategy should be a short narrative that explains how the company will win in the market by investing in key product areas.
2. **Teams respond with a proposed plan.** Teams need to read through leadership's plan and fill in the details for each

product area. A team's plan includes the vision and strategy, a list of OKRs and key projects, resources required, and risks and dependencies.

3. **Leadership shares an integrated plan.** Leadership uses each team's plan to flesh out the overall company plan. This plan includes information on which product areas are being funded, goals and timelines for each area, and which investments were cut and why.

4. **Teams confirm their buy-in.** Leadership shares a draft of the overall plan with the teams and ensure that team leads are bought in and ready to execute. This involves getting more feedback from the teams and iterating before sharing the plan broadly with the entire company.

Can you describe an individual PM's role in this planning process?

As an individual PM, you are responsible for driving the roadmap for your team (step 2) based on leadership's guidance. To do that, you need to have a well-defined vision and strategy that clearly outlines how your team will contribute to the company's priorities. Ideally, your strategy will have three pillars that you want your team to invest in.

Once you have these pillars, coming up with individual features to build is a matter of ideation, prioritization, and communication.

- **Ideation:** Start by gathering ideas from everyone on the team. Run a brainstorm meeting and meet with team members to give everyone a chance to share their ideas. Collect these ideas into a single document and organize it based on your team's strategic pillars.
- **Prioritization:** Prioritize ideas using three criteria: 1) Expected impact; 2) Cost; and 3) Risk. I suggest following the 70/20/10 rule: Roughly 70% of resources should go to low-risk, immediate impact work. Roughly 20% should go to

risky, long-term bets. And roughly 10% should go to delightful features that the team is excited about building.

- **Communication:** Communication is really important throughout the planning process. When drafting your roadmap, get feedback from your team and bring them along on the journey. Once your team and stakeholders are bought-in, share your roadmap and strategy widely. Make sure it's easy to find and the single source of truth. Always keep your roadmap updated when things change (e.g. dates, priorities, blockers).

Any other advice on roadmap planning for product managers?

Here are a few more tips for planning:

1. **Begin with the problem.** Crafting and aligning on a problem statement with your team is the single most important step for planning. A great problem statement starts with the user need.
2. **Focus.** To design a plan that has a real chance of success, you need to put your resources behind a small number of bets (ideally no more than 3). If you spread your priorities like peanut butter, your most impactful ideas won't receive the funding they need to thrive.
3. **Start early.** Think about what your team should build in the next quarter long before the planning process begins. Most successful teams get way ahead of planning and accurately anticipate leadership asks.
4. **Listen.** Listen to your teammates and talk with customers to gather the best ideas for your roadmap. Review past data-dives and research findings to understand the most impactful areas that you should invest in.
5. **Get buy-in from teams you will depend on.** Make sure teams you depend on see and buy into your plan early.

PART III

GETTING THE JOB

There are two significant hurdles to getting your first product manager job if you have limited product experience. First, you need to reach the interview stage as many recruiters will screen out non-PM candidates. Second, you need to stand out during the interview.

Passing these hurdles won't be easy, but that's what part three of this book is about. We'll start by walking through how you can prepare to transition to a product management role and reach the interview stage at the right company. We'll then prep you for the three most common types of PM interviews—product sense, execution, and behavioral—with frameworks and example answers for each. Finally, we'll close with some suggestions on how you can excel in your first 30 days as a new product manager.

20

PREPARING FOR THE TRANSITION

You should start preparing for the transition at least a few months before applying for PM jobs. Here are five steps that you can follow:

1. Be honest with yourself
2. Practice the principles
3. Start shipping
4. Do your research
5. Build a network

Be Honest with Yourself

Interviewers want to hire product managers who can clearly articulate why they want the role and what their strengths and weaknesses are.

Start by reflecting on why you want to be a PM. Do you genuinely care about customers and want to make their lives easier? Do you get satisfaction from growing metrics? Do you enjoy aligning people around a shared goal? These are all excellent reasons. On the other hand, if you want to be in charge (product managers work through influence) or enjoy being left alone (influencing others requires meetings), then the role probably isn't the best fit for you.

Once you know why you want to be a PM, write down the strengths and weaknesses that are relevant for job. In part one of this book, we discussed how you could discover your strengths and weaknesses by reflecting after successes and setbacks. Here's a quick recap:

- **Your strengths** are activities that you're both good at and enjoy doing. For example, some people are great at execution and can balance multiple projects efficiently. Others are better at resolving team conflicts or have in-depth knowledge in a particular field. Whatever your strengths are, you need to highlight them in interviews. For example, my strength was domain expertise in live streaming from working at Facebook. As a result, Twitter was willing to take a bet on me to manage a similar video product.
- **Your weaknesses** can be uncovered by finding a common thread through your past setbacks. Hiring managers want to know how you handle adversity, so a common interview question is, "Tell me about a time when you failed or had a conflict." Prepare for this question by writing down stories about your past failures and learnings. Often, I've found that strengths taken too far can become weaknesses. For example, I received negative feedback in a performance review because I had a strong sense of urgency (a strength) that too often came off as impatience with others (a weakness).

Once you've had a chance to reflect on your strengths and weaknesses, try to validate them by talking to people that you trust. This step is critical because your self-assessment might be very different from how other people perceive you. Your goal should be to get the most accurate picture of yourself so that you can confidently describe what you excel in and what you're working on to interviewers.

Practice the Principles

Interviewers want to hire PMs who have clear examples of when they took ownership, resolved conflicts, and empowered people. Start gathering these examples now by practicing the PM principles that we covered in part one of this book:

1. **Take ownership** of your work and relationships. Stay humble and be the first to admit mistakes and address problems.
2. **Prioritize and execute** on solving the most important problems first, whether that's building a relationship with a coworker or getting an important project done.
3. **Start with why** when communicating with others. Have empathy for their problems and try to align on a shared goal early.
4. **Find the truth** by vetting important decisions with other knowledgeable people.
5. **Be radically transparent** and build caring relationships with the people around you.
6. **Be honest with yourself** by setting clear goals, reflecting after successes and setbacks, and seeking feedback from others.

Practicing the principles above will not only give you great stories to tell in your product management interviews but will also improve your everyday life.

Start Shipping

Interviewers want to hire PMs who have a track record of shipping successful products. This creates a chicken-and-egg problem as people trying to transition to product often don't have this track record. There are three ways to start shipping even if you're not a PM:

- If you work with product managers in an adjacent role (e.g., designer, engineer, analyst, or marketer), then get more involved with the product side. We'll cover this in detail in the next chapter.
- If you don't work with product managers at all, then consider doing a side project. Side projects include participating in hackathons, making a personal website, or writing a blog. When you're working on your side project, follow the product development process that we covered in part two of this book. For example, if you're writing a blog, seek to understand your readers first, and then write about topics that matter to them. This way, when you're discussing your side project in a PM interview, you can frame it using the product development process (e.g., understanding the customer problem and the goal before identifying a solution).
- Finally, you can start shipping by signing up for a professional product course (e.g. General Assembly, Product School). If you're starting from scratch, picking up core product management skills and shipping a few projects at a product course can't hurt. Just keep in mind that these courses are often expensive and not required for making a successful transition.

Do Your Research

Interviewers want to hire PMs who have taken the time to research the company and the role. I can't tell you how often I've interviewed candidates who don't have a clear answer for "Why do you want to work here?" A little research goes a long way.

Here's how you can research the companies that you're interested in:

- Use the company's products and talk to the company's

customers. Write down your thoughts about how the product is meeting customer needs and where the gaps are.

- Follow the company and its executives on Twitter. Thoughtfully replying to their tweets is another way to build your network.
- Find public reports and recent news about the company. As you read these reports, write down the company's mission, strategy, and metrics.

Capture your research in a document and write down the problems that you'll tackle first if you were to join the company. If you can write a crisp document, bring it to your interview. Most candidates rarely do any research about the company, so a well-written document will impress your interviewers and help you stand out.

Build a Network

Interviewers want to hire PMs recommended by people they trust. If you don't have great product experience, a recommendations from a seasoned PM at a company will help you get your foot in the door.

That's why building a network is critical if you're trying to transition to product. To build a network, use LinkedIn or Twitter to find people who work at companies that interest you. Whenever possible, ask a mutual friend to connect you to these people. If you don't have a mutual friend, don't be afraid to reach out to people directly. The trick is to make sure your inquiry provides some value to the person you're contacting. Here's how you can do that:

1. Find a company that you're interested in.
2. Research the company and, if possible, use the product.
3. Write a short, personal e-mail to someone in the company. People's emails are usually (first name)@(company name) or (first name).(last name)@(company name). In your e-mail,

suggest some product ideas before asking about job opportunities.

Here's an example e-mail:

> Dear Ivan,
>
> I love using Notion to manage my daily to-do list and take notes during meetings. I want to be able to select multiple items in my to-do list and delete more than one item at a time (I usually clear my to-do list at the end of each day).
>
> I wrote a blog post about my love for Notion, and here's my LinkedIn. If you're hiring, do you know of any opportunities where I can be a good fit?
>
> I am looking forward to hearing from you and thanks for making a great product.

You can see how the above e-mail might be more effective than "Dear Ivan, how do I get a job at your company?" If you still feel hesitant about cold e-mailing people, here's a quick story:

> When Steve Jobs was a teenager, he cold-called Hewlett-Packard's co-founder Bill Hewlett for some electronic parts. Bill was so impressed by Steve's audacity that he offered him a job soon after. When asked about this years later, Steve said: "Most people don't get these experiences because they never ask."[1]

The point is, you should aggressively reach out to people at companies that interest you in a way that provides value to them.

A Closing Note

You may be wondering why none of the steps above include

preparing for product manager interviews. We'll cover interview preparation later, but you should get ready to make the transition well before you have your first product interview.

21

MAKING THE TRANSITION

You've prepared for the transition and now you're ready to land your first PM job. There are three common ways to become a product manager:

1. Transfer internally.
2. Join an entry-level PM program.
3. Hustle and find a company that's willing to take a chance on you.

Transfer Internally

If you already work with product managers in your current job, then your best bet is to transfer internally. Start by using your superpower to get more involved in the product side:

1. If you're a designer, use your designs to bring to life a vision of the ideal product experience. Inspire your team with that vision and help your PM prioritize what to build.
2. If you're an engineer, use your technical knowledge to help your PM evaluate trade-offs when defining the product.

3. If you're an analyst, use your understanding of product metrics to identify opportunity areas. Help your PM tackle these areas by defining experiments and how you'll measure success.

4. If you're a marketer, use your project management and customer empathy skills to help your PM drive execution and alignment earlier in the product development process.

While you're doing the above, find a senior or director level PM who's willing to back your transition internally. Make sure you meet that person at least once a month to provide regular updates. Once your sponsor thinks you're ready to make the transition, start preparing for interviews (look up internal resources on how the company interviews product managers) and take the leap.

One tricky thing about internal transfers is setting the right expectations with your current manager. If you have a great relationship with your manager, you can be honest with her that you want to transition and work with her to make it happen. However, if your manager thinks you're underperforming or is insecure about losing you, you may want to tell her only after you're ready for PM interviews.

Join an Entry-Level PM Program

Large tech companies such as Google, Facebook, and Amazon often have associate product manager and PM internship programs. These programs are competitive, with recruiting focused on hiring students from top universities. It doesn't hurt to apply, but if you don't get in, it's not the end of the world.

Many other companies have entry-level product manager opportunities but don't do a good job advertising them on their career website. To find these opportunities, you need to hustle.

Hustle and Find a Company That's Willing to Take a Chance on You

If you can't transfer internally or join an entry-level PM program, then you need to hustle to land a product manager job. That means knowing your strengths and weaknesses, doing your research, and building your network.

For example, recently, an MBA student reached out to me on LinkedIn because I went to the same school a few years ago. After speaking to her on the phone, I submitted a job referral for her at my company. She wasn't able to land a full-time product manager job, but we offered her a three-month internship that could convert to a permanent role.

Stories like the above are more common than you think, but landing your first PM job requires persistence. As you read at the beginning of this book, I failed to become a product manager multiple times before finally making the transition. Back then, I was full of self-doubt and ready to give up, but I'm glad that I didn't. If you're getting rejected or hitting a brick wall, I've found these words of wisdom helpful:

- Jim Carrey: "You can fail at what you don't want, so you might as well take a chance at doing what you love."[1]
- Chris Hadfield: "I decided a long time ago that I wanted to be an astronaut. Let's head in the direction that I like...even if I don't make it all the way. Don't measure success by one thing at the end, measure success by each of the small things along the way."[2]

If you know that you want to be a product manager, then keep getting better and don't give up until you achieve your goal.

22

FINDING THE RIGHT COMPANY

Finding the right company to join can have a significant impact on your career, so take the time to research your options before making a decision. If you're a new product manager, then my advice is to optimize for learning by joining a market leader or a high-growth company. Be wary of joining startups that haven't found product-market fit or companies that are struggling to grow.

Market Leader

If you're a brand new product manager, then I recommend that you join a market leader.

Working at a market leader has many advantages. Companies such as Facebook, Amazon, Google, Airbnb, and others not only pay well but also provide a great brand on your resume. But the main advantage of working at a market leader is learning firsthand how PMs at the most successful companies ship products. Market leaders have an army of senior PMs whom you can follow. From Amazon's working backward process to Facebook's impact-driven culture, the best practices that you learn at these companies will be invaluable for the rest of your career.

Working at a market leader also has disadvantages. As a new PM, you'll likely be optimizing a single feature. Similarly, you'll spend a lot of time in meetings seeking alignment with other teams and your management chain to get anything done.

Many of the best practices in this book are from my experience working for market leaders, so I admit I'm somewhat biased. But I don't think you can go wrong with spending a few years shipping products while picking up best practices at one of these companies. If, however, you find that the job is not challenging you anymore, then it's probably time to move on to a high-growth company.

High-Growth

If you already have a few years of product management experience, then I recommend that you join a high-growth company.

High-growth companies have strong product-market fit and are rapidly scaling. The list of high-growth companies is changing all the time, but Wealthfront's annual career launching companies list[1] is an excellent place to start.

The main advantage of working for a high-growth company is that your responsibilities will scale as the company scales. Since high-growth companies can't hire fast enough, you'll likely have broad product scope on day one. You'll learn how to scale users and revenue, a unique skill that can be both personally and financially rewarding. Product managers have made fortunes by jumping from one high-growth company to another. Finally, if you prove yourself, you'll likely get management and leadership opportunities early—both of which could take longer to find at market leaders.

The main disadvantage of joining a high-growth company is that people won't have time to teach you how to be a good product manager. Instead, you'll be expected to hit the ground running on day 1. The problems that you'll be asked to solve will be ambiguous (e.g., help us grow), and you'll get little support. It could be a challenge (but not impossible) for new product managers to adjust to the often-chaotic environments at these companies.

A final note about high-growth companies—try to join them when they are just starting to scale. During the interview process, ask to take a look at the company's numbers. You want to make sure that their growth is real and that you're not joining a company that's in a turnaround situation.

Turnaround

A turnaround is a company that has found some product-market fit but has stopped growing. Maybe their addressable market isn't large enough, or perhaps there are some other issues. When you talk to a turnaround, they'll usually try to sell you that the company's upcoming initiatives will push it into a high-growth stage.

Turnarounds can work out, but be wary. If turnarounds don't succeed, they'll either stagnant or shrink, neither of which are great for your PM career. Look at the numbers and the product roadmap, and make sure that you believe that a turnaround can happen before you accept an offer from one of these companies.

Early-Stage

I define early-stage as a company that's still trying to find product-market fit and is not yet ready to scale. I do not recommend that junior product managers join these companies, with a few exceptions.

The benefit of joining an early-stage company is that you'll join a small team with one overriding goal: to find and retain customers. You'll wear multiple hats, from engineer to designer to sales and more, and it could be thrilling to work with your team to iterate toward product-market fit.

However, being a product manager at an early-stage company comes with many risks. First, you need to build a great relationship with the founder(s) if you want to influence the product. Second, most early-stage companies don't find product-market fit before funding runs out. Finally, if the company doesn't have senior PMs, it'll be more challenging for you to pick up best practices.

So, joining an early-stage company is a gamble. Personally, unless you think the company has huge potential or you have a solid relationship with the founder, you'll likely be better off being a founder yourself than being the PM hire at an early-stage company.

Optimize to Get the PM Job Title as Soon as Possible

Suppose that you receive an offer from your dream company, but it's not a product manager role. You also have a PM offer from a company that you're less excited about. Which offer should you take?

People trying to transition to product management often have to make this decision. Of course, you should research each company and your future manager before deciding. You should also keep interviewing to see if you can be a PM at a company that you're more excited about. If you only have these two options, I would take the PM role instead of joining your dream company as a non-PM.

Transitioning to product management internally is not guaranteed and typically takes at least a year. During that time, you'll get frustrated trying to do PM work in a non-PM function, and you could end up doing your real job poorly as a result. The best way to optimize for learning is to get practical PM experience as soon as possible, even if the company is less appealing.

There's one exception to this, and that's the popular phrase: "If you're offered a seat on a rocket ship, you don't ask what seat." If you're joining a high-growth company, then consider taking an offer for an adjacent function even if you can't be a PM right away. High-growth companies are scaling rapidly and are always looking for talent. If you do great work and prove yourself, you can probably make the transition to PM sooner rather than later.

Get to Know Your Manager Before Joining

One last note: Take the time to get to know your future manager before joining a company. Surveys show that bad managers are the number one reason people leave companies, and this is even more true for product managers. A manager who works hard to make you successful is a fantastic ally. In contrast, a manager who makes unreasonable demands and cares more about his career than yours can be a nightmare. Get to know your manager and make sure that you can work well with him or her. In many cases, who your manager is matters more than the company's reputation or brand.

23

ACING YOUR PM INTERVIEWS

All the steps that we covered so far will help you get your foot in the door, but you still need to pass the product management interview loop. This loop generally includes three types of interviews:

1. **Product sense:** Can this person turn an ambiguous customer problem into a great product?
2. **Execution:** Can this person prioritize and execute to get things done?
3. **Behavioral:** Can this person inspire a team and lead a project?

Before we dive into each type, here are a few best practices that apply to all three interviews:

1. **Do your research.** Research the company and your interviewers ahead of time. Write down key facts about the company (e.g., customers, mission, strategy, competition) and what you like or dislike about the company's products. Look up your interviewers on LinkedIn to understand their background. Most candidates don't do research, so if you can

recite the company's mission or connect with an interviewer, you'll stand out.

2. **Show enthusiasm.** Smile and show enthusiasm during each interview. Talk about what genuinely excites you about working at the company, whether it's the company's mission, products, or culture.

3. **Have a conversation.** Your interview should be a conversation between you and the interviewer, not a monologue. Talk through your ideas out loud and check in with the interviewer regularly. Try to build rapport and connection with the interviewer.

Ultimately, if you feel like you had a fun and engaging conversation with the interviewer and both of you learned something new—then you probably did pretty well.

With that overview, let's move on to discussing how you can ace the product sense interview.

24

PRODUCT SENSE INTERVIEW

The product sense interview evaluates whether you can identify a customer problem, tie that problem to a company goal, and define a solution. Your interviewer will begin the conversation by providing a problem statement (e.g., "Design a product for people to find apartments.") before letting you drive the discussion.

What Your Interviewer Is Looking For

During the product sense interview, your interviewer is looking for:

1. **Structure:** Do you start with defining a customer problem before diving into a solution? Can you tie the problem to a company goal?
2. **Vision:** Can you present a clear and inspiring product vision? Is your vision based on the most important benefit that you can deliver to the customer?
3. **Creativity:** Can you brainstorm multiple problems and solutions, including out of the box ideas that the interviewer hasn't thought about?

4. **Prioritization:** Can you prioritize problems and solutions to identify what to tackle first?

5. **Communication:** Do you walk the interviewer through your thinking by talking out loud and using the whiteboard? Do you try to reach alignment with your interviewer each step of the way? Can you refine your solution based on information that the interviewer provides?

Product Sense Framework

You should take a structured approach when answering product sense questions. Just like building a product, you should start the interview with the problem and goal before diving into the solution:

Ask clarifying questions and explain your approach.

1. Problem

a) Who are the customers?

b) What problems do they have?

2. Goal

a) How do these problems relate to the company's mission?

b) What metric are we trying to improve?

Summarize the problem and the goal.

3. Solution

a) Map out the user journey

b) Brainstorm solutions

c) Discuss trade-offs and prioritize

d) Wireframe the MVP

Summarize the problem, goal, and solution.

Let's walk through an example interview by applying the framework above.

———

Product Sense Example

Airbnb wants to let people book event spaces like photo studios and outdoor lounges. As the events product manager, how would you bring this product category to market?

Ask clarifying questions.

<u>Candidate</u>: Thank you! If you don't mind, I'd like to ask a few questions. First, are there event spaces listed on Airbnb today?

<u>Interviewer</u>: No, but there are some homes listed on Airbnb that could qualify as event spaces.

<u>Candidate</u>: Good to know, is there a type of event space that we want to focus on first?

<u>Interviewer</u>: I think that's up to you to decide.

Explain your approach.

<u>Candidate</u>: Ok, here's how I plan to tackle this problem. First, I want to understand our customers and their pain points better. Second, let's discuss how addressing these pain points can help Airbnb achieve its goals. Finally, I'd like to brainstorm solutions and then define the MVP with you. Does that sound good?

<u>Interviewer</u>: That sounds great.

<u>*Whiteboard:*</u>

1. *Problem*

2. *Goal*

3. Solution

The candidate set up a clear framework upfront by talking out loud (First...second...finally) and using the whiteboard. She'll use this framework as a guide for the rest of the interview.

1. Problem

Candidate: Great, so I think there are two customers here, event space hosts and event organizers.

Hosts don't want their spaces to go unused, especially during non-peak times (e.g., a restaurant in the afternoon). They want to earn income and meet people by finding organizers to rent out their spaces.

Organizers want to find spaces to celebrate events like offsites and parties with their guests.

Today, hosts and organizers rely on word of mouth, online searches, phone calls, and in-person visits to find each other and book a space. This process is time-consuming and inefficient.

Whiteboard:

1. Problem

Hosts: Rent space to earn income and meet people.

Organizers: Find spaces to celebrate offsites, parties, etc.

Finding and booking an event space is inefficient: Search / word of mouth → phone calls / in-person visits.

Candidate: Are there any problems that I missed?

Interviewer: What about our existing hosts?

Candidate: Yes, that's a great point. As you mentioned, some of our existing hosts already have event spaces listed as homes on Airbnb. They could also have spaces that they haven't listed yet. I think current hosts have the same goals as event space owners: they want to earn income by renting out their space for events. Come to think of it, helping existing hosts rent out their space may be an excellent way for us to enter this market.

Interviewer: Great, let's keep going.

The candidate started by identifying the customers (there are usually several types) and their pain points. By checking with the interviewer, the candidate was also able to identify a customer segment that she missed (existing hosts). Remember that the interviewer wants to help you succeed, so check in regularly to give him or her an opportunity to provide input.

2. Goal

Candidate: Ok, now let's think about how helping hosts rent out spaces to organizers helps Airbnb.

Airbnb's vision is to create a world where everyone can belong anywhere. Adding event spaces will bring us closer to our vision by helping existing hosts earn more income. It will also attract new hosts and guests to our platform. From a metrics perspective, I think we would want to measure both growth (number of event bookings) and customer satisfaction (ratings and reviews).

I know we're focused on defining the MVP, but let's imagine what the future could look like for a minute. Long term, we can give hosts tools to help organizers plan their entire event and trip. For example, a host could offer add-on services like catering and allow an organizer to book an event space, home, and experience together as a package.

Whiteboard:

2. Goal

Vision: Anyone belong anywhere. Plan the entire event and trip.

Event spaces: Helps hosts earn $, attract new hosts/guests.

Metrics: Growth (bookings), satisfaction (ratings).

The candidate was able to tie the customer problem to Airbnb's vision and key metrics, which she researched before the interview. As bonus points, she also painted a vision of what event spaces could unlock for Airbnb's business as a whole to give the interviewer a sense of her strategic thinking.

Interviewer: That's very interesting, I like how you're thinking about trips as a whole and not just event spaces. But let's go back to the immediate goal: Would you focus on growing supply or demand to grow event bookings?

Candidate: Well to grow event bookings, we need both hosts and organizers. Do we know how many existing hosts already have event spaces listed as homes?

Interviewer: Let's assume that that are very few event spaces listed as homes, but a lot of existing hosts have event spaces that they haven't listed yet.

Candidate: That sounds like an opportunity for us! I think we should focus on supply—specifically, getting our existing hosts to list quality event spaces on Airbnb. Once hosts list their spaces, we can promote these listings on our platform to encourage organizers to book events. Do you agree?

Interviewer: Yes, I think that makes sense.

By establishing a dialogue with the interviewer and asking questions, the candidate was able to unlock the insight that many existing hosts on Airbnb haven't listed their event space.

Summarize the problem and the goal.

Candidate: Great. Before we discuss the solution, let's summarize the problem and the goal. We want to focus on helping our existing hosts list their event spaces to earn more income. Our goal is to grow bookings and achieve high customer ratings.

Whiteboard:

Help existing hosts list spaces for organizers to find.

Interviewer: Sounds good to me.

Summarize the problem and goal in a few crisp sentences before discussing the solution. Product managers do this all the time when meeting with stakeholders, so it's a good practice during the interview as well.

3. Solution

Candidate: Ok now let's think about how we can solve this problem. To begin, I'd like to map out the user journey for event space hosts:

Whiteboard:

Solution

Host user journey with event spaces:

a) Awareness and intent to list space

b) List space

c) Find organizer

d) Accept bookings

e) Get paid

f) Attend event (optional)

g) Thank organizer / ask for ratings

Candidate: Since we're focused on helping existing hosts list spaces,

I think we should tackle the first two steps of this journey first. Let's think about how we can improve host awareness of event spaces and make it easier for them to list their space.

The candidate mapped out the full user journey before prioritizing the steps that she'll tackle first. She was able to easily explain why she prioritized the first two steps of the user journey because she had summarized the problem and goal earlier.

Whiteboard:

a) Awareness and intent to list space

We should target hosts with:

- Event space type homes (e.g. lofts)

- Event space type user profiles (e.g. restaurant owner)

- Good ratings and reviews

Channels: E-mail, in-product notification, referrals, search ads

b) List space

Listing details:

- Type of space

- Type of event

- # of attendees

- Location

- Amenities

- Photos

- Price per hour

- Hours available

Interviewer: How will you prioritize these ideas for our MVP?

Candidate: Ok, let's think this through step by step.

To grow supply, I think we should send an e-mail to hosts who have event space type homes (e.g., lofts) and profiles (e.g., restaurant owner). We should also target our top-rated hosts first to make sure that we have quality event space listings when launching this new category. I chose e-mail as our channel because we may have hosts who are inactive on Airbnb but still have fantastic event spaces to list.

For listing an event space, I think we only need to make a few modifications to the existing home-listing process. We need to add space type, event type, number of attendees, price/hour, and hours available. The rest of the process we can repurpose from the home listings flow.

Whiteboard:

a) Awareness and intent to list space

We should target hosts with:

- Event space type homes (e.g. lofts)

- Event space type user profiles (e.g. restaurant owner)

- Good ratings and reviews

Channels: E-mail, in product notification, referrals, search ads

b) List space

Listing details:

- Type of space

- Type of event

- # of attendees

- ~~Location~~

- ~~Amenities~~

- ~~Photos~~

- Price / hour

- Hours available

- ~~Get bookings~~

- ~~Accept / deny~~

- ~~Chat~~

- ~~Insights~~

The candidate brainstormed an extensive list of ideas before prioritizing what to build for the MVP. She explained her rationale out loud and also crossed out ideas on the whiteboard as she deprioritized them.

Interviewer: Do you think this MVP is good enough for all types of events?

Candidate: Probably not. We should start with simple events like team off-sites and parties. A complex event like a wedding comes with high expectations and multiple vendors, so we shouldn't tackle these events until later.

Interviewer: Makes sense. What about the demand side?

Candidate: On the demand side, we need to make organizers aware that they can now book event spaces on Airbnb. We also need to make it easy for them to find and book spaces. Let's let them select an event space category first, then filter by event type, number of attendees, and other fields. We can use our existing messaging and payment tools when the organizer is ready to book a space.

The candidate did not get flustered or defensive when the interviewer asked follow up questions. Instead, she listened carefully to the interviewer's input and was thoughtful in addressing any concerns.

Summarize the problem, goal, and solution.

Interviewer: Ok, do you want to summarize everything?

Candidate: Yes! Event space hosts want to earn income by finding organizers to book their space.

Entering the event spaces market will help our existing hosts earn more income and attract new hosts and guests to our platform. Long term, our goal is to be the end-to-end provider of events and trips. For this launch, we'll measure success through bookings and customer ratings.

To enter this market, we decided to focus on helping our existing hosts list their space. We will send a targeted e-mail to existing hosts to encourage them to register their spaces. We will also modify our home-listing process for event spaces and allow organizers to find these spaces on Airbnb easily. If we execute well, our MVP should give us a set of quality event space listings that we can promote on Airbnb for event organizers to find.

The candidate was able to close the interview with a strong summary because she organized everything on the whiteboard and walked through the case in a structured way.

―――――

THE EXAMPLE above should give you an idea of how you can demonstrate structure, vision, creativity, prioritization, and communication in a product sense interview.

25

EXECUTION INTERVIEW

The execution interview evaluates your ability to set goals, make effective trade-offs, and identify root causes.

What Your Interviewer Is Looking For

During the execution interview, your interviewer is looking for:

1. **Goal setting:** Can you define a goal metric for the product that aligns with customer and company goals? Can you evaluate whether your goal is a good one?
2. **Trade-offs:** Can you align on goals with another team? How do you make decisions and navigate trade-offs?
3. **Root cause:** Can you take a broad problem and break it down into smaller pieces to identify the root cause?

Execution Frameworks

Just like the product sense interview, you should answer execution questions in a structured way. Here are several frameworks that you can use:

Setting Goals

> **Ask clarifying questions and explain your approach.**
>
> 1. **Problem**
>
> 2. **Company**
>
> 3. **Solution**
>
> a) Map out the user journey
>
> b) Brainstorm metrics
>
> c) Select a goal metric
>
> 4. **Evaluate the goal**
>
> a) Customer and company goals?
>
> b) Short-term or long-term goal?
>
> c) Can it be gamed?
>
> d) Can you team drive it?
>
> **Summarize.**

Evaluating Trade-Offs

There are many different ways to answer trade-off questions. Here are a few best practices based on what we learned in previous chapters:

1. **Start with why.** Try to align on shared goals first.
2. **Gather more information.** Understand the pros and cons of each trade-off (e.g. can you run a simple experiment as a path forward?)
3. **Disagree and commit or escalate.** If two people or teams don't have shared goals, it becomes tough to agree on a path forward. In these situations, you need to either disagree and commit or escalate to your management chain.

Root Cause Analysis

If a metric declined, evaluate:

1. Logging issue

2. Time period

3. Platform

4. Location

5. Externalities

6. Customer journey

Summarize.

Let's walk through an example interview that uses all three frameworks above.

———

Goal Setting Example

You're the product manager for Facebook Groups. What goal will you set?

Ask clarifying questions.

Candidate: Thank you! By groups, are you referring to public groups in the main Facebook app or private groups that I can form with friends on Messenger?

Interviewer: Good question. I'm referring to the groups product in the main Facebook app, but these groups can be both public or private.

Explain your approach.

Candidate: Thanks! Ok, here's how I plan to tackle this problem. First, I want to better understand our customers and their pain points. Second, I want to know why Groups matters to Facebook. Third, I'd like to walk through the user journey and brainstorm a possible goal metric. Finally, I'd like to evaluate whether the metric makes sense. Does that sound good?

Interviewer: Yes, let's proceed.

Whiteboard:

1. Problem

2. Company

3. Solution

4. Goal

1. Problem

Candidate: Great, so I think there are two types of customers for Facebook groups: creators who make groups and members who join and participate in groups. There are also many different types of groups. For example, I'm part of a new dad group where I get a lot of baby advice and a shopping group for a brand that I like.

At a high level, I think people create and join groups to be part of a community that shares a common interest or identity. Do you agree?

Interviewer: Yes, that makes sense.

Whiteboard:

1. Problem

Customers: Creators, members

Types of groups: Interest, commerce, local, friend

Summary: Be part of a community that shares a common interest or identity.

2. Company

Candidate: Ok, now let's discuss why Groups matters to Facebook. Facebook's mission is to bring the world closer together. Groups is a key part of this mission because it brings people together around a common interest or identity—whether that's a group for new parents, shoppers, or people from a local neighborhood. At a time when social media is getting attention for dividing people, I think Groups can help people create and be part of communities that matter to them.

In terms of metrics, can you tell me what overall metrics the company tracks?

Interviewer: What do you think?

Candidate: In the past, I would have said metrics like time spent. But I think what Facebook cares about now is helping people have meaningful interactions. This metric directly relates to Facebook's mission to bring the world closer together.

Interviewer: Yes, well, we still care about time spent, but we want people to spend time on Facebook forming meaningful connections and interactions.

Candidate: Ok sounds good. Let me write this down.

Whiteboard:

2. Company

FB: Bring the world closer together.

Metric: Meaningful interactions

3. Solution

Candidate: Great, now before we pick a metric to set a goal for, I just want to map out the full user journey for groups.

Whiteboard:

Journey / metrics

1. Create groups

2. Discover / join groups

3. Read group posts

4. Interact in groups

<u>Candidate</u>: Now I'd like to brainstorm metrics for each step of the journey.

Whiteboard:

1. Create groups

a) Daily active group creators

b) # of groups created

2. Discover / join groups

a) # group joins

3. Read group posts

a) # people who create group content

b) # people who read group posts

c) Time spent reading group posts

4. Interact in groups

a) CTR for link and photo group posts

b) Likes / comments / shares on group posts

c) Hide story actions for groups

4. Evaluate the goal.

<u>Candidate</u>: As you can see, there are a lot of metrics here. Let's use

the following criteria to evaluate which goal metric we should choose.

Whiteboard:

4. Evaluate metric

a) Customer / company goals?

b) Short-term or long-term goal?

c) Can metric be gamed?

d) Can the team drive it?

Candidate: First, we should choose a metric that aligns with customer and company goals. Earlier, we mentioned that both group creators and members want to be part of a community that shares a common interest or identity. We also know that Facebook's mission is to bring the world closer together, with meaningful interactions as a goal metric. Given all this, I would want to look at the "interact in groups" step of the user journey. Of the metrics that we brainstormed for this step, I think measuring comments on group posts is interesting. Comments usually take more thought than likes and shares and are more likely to be a meaningful interaction. Instead of just looking at total comments, I think setting a goal for daily active group commenters makes sense. We want as many people to have meaningful interactions as possible.

Interviewer: That's interesting. I understand why you think comments might be meaningful, but there are also a lot of comments on Facebook and other platforms that aren't meaningful.

Candidate: That's a good point. Facebook does require users to give their real identity, so comments in Facebook groups should be more meaningful than comments on other platforms. That said, I think we should track the number of comment likes, hides, and reports as secondary metrics to monitor comment quality.

Interviewer: Ok let's keep going.

Candidate: Next, let's look at whether this is a short-term or long-term goal. Given that there are already a lot of groups active on Facebook, I think selecting daily group commenters as a short-term goal is OK. If, on the other hand, there aren't a lot of groups, then I would probably pick a goal earlier in the user journey like daily groups created.

Interviewer: That's fair.

Candidate: Now, let's think about how we can game daily group commenters. We already discussed that not all comments are good and that we should monitor negative signals like comment hides or user reports. Just from using Reddit, I know that having moderators is critical to ensuring that discussions remain productive and on topic. I would want to measure daily active moderators as another metric.

Interviewer: You're measuring a lot of metrics. I want to make sure that the daily group commenters metric is still your goal metric?

Candidate: Yes, I think so. Comment hides, user reports, and daily moderators are useful health metrics to monitor, but our goal metric should still be daily commenters.

Summarize.

Interviewer: Ok sounds good. Do you want to wrap this up?

Candidate: Yes. The mission for Facebook Groups is to help people create and be part of communities that matter to them. This mission relates directly to Facebook's mission to bring the world closer together. After mapping out the user journey for groups, we decided to use daily group commenters as our goal metric. This goal ties directly to Facebook's mission and helps grow meaningful interactions. However, we want to make sure that we're also monitoring the quality of comments. We will track comment likes, hides, reports, and daily moderators as secondary metrics.

Trade-Off Example

Ok, now imagine that you're trying to grow daily active commenters for groups by surfacing group posts in News Feed. When trying to do this, you come into conflict with the video team who wants to grow video engagement on Facebook. What do you do?

Candidate: Hmm, that's a good question. How does the video team measure engagement?

Interviewer: They measure engagement using video watch time and the number of comments on video posts.

Candidate: Ok. How about the News Feed team?

Interviewer: The News Feed team cares a lot about meaningful interactions since News Feed is the most critical surface on Facebook. To them, a meaningful interaction is either a comment or a reaction (like).

Candidate: Thank you! So, it sounds like the trade-off is this: if we promote group posts in News Feed, then video posts could get less visibility. There isn't a way to encourage both video and group posts?

Interviewer: Let's assume that there isn't.

Candidate: Ok, first, I would try to align all three teams on the same goal metric. It sounds they all care about growing comments as a goal.

Interviewer: Yes that's true, but the video team also cares about watch time and the News Feed team also cares about reactions.

Candidate: I think we should ask the video and News Feed teams to let us run an experiment to promote group posts in Feed. For this experiment, we'll set growing the number of daily active commenters as the primary goal while also monitoring video watch time and reactions. If daily active commenters grow significantly while the other two metrics are stable, I think we should be able to ship the experiment.

Interviewer: Let's say comments grow significantly, but video watch time declines. As a result, the video team is not happy.

Candidate: In that case, I would explore two paths:

1. Run another experiment promoting group video posts to see if it improves both watch time and comments.

2. Explore other channels (e.g. notifications) to grow group posts without coming into conflict with the video team.

Interviewer: Ok, let's say these two options don't work out and the video team is still blocking your launch. Now what?

Candidate: At this point, I would work with the video team to escalate this decision to someone who is a leader for both teams. The problem here is that both sides have different goals. I would rather escalate quickly and get an answer instead of arguing back and forth between two teams with misaligned goals.

————

Root Cause Example

Great. Now imagine that daily active commenters have declined 10% over the past month. How would you understand why?

Candidate: Thanks. I would work with my analyst to investigate the following:

Whiteboard:

1. Logging issue

2. Time period

3. Platform

4. Location

5. Externalities

6. Customer journey

Candidate: My first question would be, is this a logging issue?

Interviewer: Let's assume that logging is correct.

Candidate: Got it. Now let's look at the time period. You mentioned that commenters declined over 30% in the most recent month. Could this be due to seasonality? I would look at the same month last year as a comparison.

Interviewer: There is some seasonality but it doesn't really explain the 10% drop.

Candidate: Interesting. When during the month did the 10% drop happen? Was it a steady drop throughout the month or did it drop drastically on one particular day?

Interviewer: After some investigation, we found that the majority of the drop came from a weekend in the middle of the month.

Candidate: Hmm, I wonder what happened that weekend? Did the drop happen across all our platforms?

Interviewer: No, the majority of the drop came from Android.

Candidate: Did something break on our Android app?

Interviewer: What do you mean?

Candidate: For example, did the Facebook app fail to load that weekend or something broke with the user journey for groups? Create groups, join groups, comment in groups, etc.

Interviewer: No, we didn't see any significant product errors during that time.

Candidate: Ok, did the drop happen in a particular region or country?

Interviewer: Yes, commenters in Brazil declined drastically.

Candidate: Very interesting. What happened in Brazil that weekend?

Interviewer: There was an election that weekend and two of our largest groups in Brazil were shut down for violating our community guidelines.

Candidate: Wow! Ok, I would look into why those groups were shut down but if that's true, then it makes sense that our commenters metric would drop.

————

BEING able to execute is a fundamental requirement for all product managers. I hope that this example interview gives you an idea of how to answer execution questions well.

26

BEHAVIORAL INTERVIEW

The behavioral interview focuses on the principles that we covered in the opening chapters of this book. Your interviewer is trying to understand if you can build and support a team, are aware of your strengths and weaknesses, and have learned from past failures and conflicts.

What Your Interviewer is Looking For

During the behavioral interview, your interviewer is looking for:

1. **Ownership:** Do you take ownership of mistakes instead of making excuses or blaming others?
2. **Self-awareness:** Are you aware of your strengths and weaknesses? How have you used your strengths and learned from your weaknesses in the past?
3. **Drive:** Do you have the conviction and determination to do what it takes to get something done?
4. **Communication:** Do you have empathy for others and try to build relationships? Do you try to resolve conflicts by thinking from the other person's point of view?

Behavioral Questions

People often list their accomplishments on their resume, but the behavioral interview is more focused on conflicts and failures than successes. For this interview, you should prepare at least five stories to answer different types of behavioral questions. When writing your stories, keep the PM principles in mind. Here's how you can answer each question using the principles:

Achievement

Question: Tell me about a time when

...you were proud of something that you did.

Answer: Talk about something that you're proud of but highlight the adversity and challenges that you faced along the way.

Failure

Question: Tell me about a time when

...you managed a product that failed.

...you failed to convince someone of an idea.

...you had to work on a weakness to be successful.

Answer: Talk about a real team failure that you were responsible for. Take ownership of how your actions contributed to the failure and the lessons that you learned.

Conflict

Question: Tell me about a time when

...you had a conflict with someone.

...your team wasn't working well together.

Answer: Talk about how you resolved a major conflict within your team, with executives, or between teams by aligning people around shared goals and seeking out the truth.

Drive

Question: Tell me about a time when

...you had to be scrappy to get something done.

...you rallied a group of people to do something.

Answer: Talk about a project where you rallied your team to go the distance by starting with why the project is important and helping your team prioritize and execute.

Behavioral Framework

A good framework to use when answering behavioral questions is the STAR method:

1. **Situation:** Describe the situation that you were in or the task that you needed to accomplish. Be sure to give enough detail for the interviewer to understand.
2. **Task:** What were you trying to achieve?
3. **Action:** Describe the actions you took to address the situation with an appropriate amount of detail and keep the focus on yourself.
4. **Result:** Describe the outcome of your actions and don't be shy about taking credit for your behavior.

When using the STAR method, your goal is not just to recount what happened, but to tell an engaging story to the interviewer. A great story has interesting characters and conflict—it shouldn't just be a dry list of facts. Let's walk through an example from my work experience.

————

Behavioral Example

Tell me about a time when you had to work on a weakness to be successful.

Situation: I think one of my strengths is a bias for action. I've always taken pride in my ability to get things done. But I had to learn to balance this trait with not making my teammates feel left out.

Task: Let me give you two examples: one where my bias for action became a weakness; and another where I applied what I learned from the first example.

Action: At Twitter, I wanted to talk to customers. I met with my partner manager and let her know that I would be reaching out to a few partners. But I didn't keep her in the loop in my conversations. I started reaching out to top partners without telling her, and she would hear from these partners that they had spoken to me. Worse, some of these partners would actually live stream talking about how they enjoyed talking to me compared to my community manager. I felt really bad about this and apologized, but the damage was done.

At Twitch, I again wanted to talk to customers and my user researcher was too busy to join me in these sessions. But this time, I spent a lot of time with her upfront to making sure that I wasn't asking leading questions. I invited her to all the calls I had in case she could join. I also reviewed my notes with her and gave her a lot of credit when I published them. She really appreciated the close collaboration.

Result: What I learned is having a bias for action does not give me an excuse to not keep my teammates in the loop. By leaving out experts like my partner manager and user researcher, I was taking a longer time to find the truth than I needed to and doing a disservice to the product.

———

PART one of this book has more examples from my work experience mapped to the PM principles. The more you can communicate how you followed or learned from the PM principles, the more successful you'll be in this interview.

27

YOUR FIRST 30 DAYS

Congratulations, you've been hired as a product manager! Your first 30 days will feel overwhelming, so here are a few tips to help you get off to a good start with your new team.

Many new PMs are eager to ship products and show impact right away. But coming in and telling your team what to do is probably the quickest way to alienate them. Instead, you should focus on building relationships, learning as much as possible, finding gaps to fill, and defining a starter project in your first 30 days.

Build Relationships

A product manager's job is to lead the people around them to solve an important customer problem. You can't lead people if you haven't built strong relationships, so getting to know your co-workers should be your top priority.

Ask your manager for a list of people with whom you should set up 1:1s. These people typically include your peers in engineering, design, analytics, and other teams. Make sure you also spend time to meet with your skip level manager and other directors and VPs. The more senior someone is, the more likely she is to have a broad strategic view of the company and the product.

During these meetings, your goal is to get to know the other person on a personal level. Here are a few questions that you can ask to get the conversation going

- How long have you been at (company)? What did you do before?
- What do you do in your current role?
- What challenges are you facing?
- How can we work together?
- Is there anything that I can do to help you now?

Be humble and show others that you're eager to learn. Take notes after each 1:1 so that you can remember the person's projects and concerns the next time you meet them.

Learn as Much as Possible

Your first 30 days is a perfect time to build a deep understanding of your team's mission, customers, and product. You will learn a lot just by talking to people, but you should also use the following channels:

- Talk to customers and read user research. It's never too early to start obsessing about customer problems.
- Get access to internal company and team dashboards. Ask an analyst or another product manager to walk you through the output and input metrics that are driving the business.
- Read monthly business reviews and product roadmaps. These documents usually include both the big picture (e.g., vision, strategy) and the team's current challenges to help you build context faster.

Find Gaps to Fill

We already discussed how you should focus on listening and learning in your first 30 days. But that doesn't mean that you can't find gaps to fill. The best way to find these gaps is to ask your teammates questions like "What challenges are you facing?" and "Is there something that I can help with now?" Look for opportunities to take care of work that your teammates don't want to do. For example, if your analyst is struggling with manual data entry or validation, offer to take that off his plate. The more annoying the work is, the more your teammate will appreciate your help.

A typical gap that I've found in most teams is note-taking and communication. Something as simple as sharing notes after meetings could bring a lot of value to your team. Also, make a habit of sharing weekly updates that document your team's highlights and lowlights. You'll be surprised at how often people are not in sync.

Define a Starter Project

As a new PM, you want to set the right expectations with your manager and team, so finding the right starter project to work on is very important. A good starter project meets the following criteria:

- You can complete it in three months or less.
- You can ship a customer-facing feature (it shouldn't be an internal-facing document).
- You can move an output metric that matters to your team.
- You can work with a few other stakeholders.
- It's not critical to your organization.

The last item in the list above may seem out of place, but I still recommend it. As a new PM, you don't want to work on something that has a lot of attention and pressure. Instead, you should ship a smaller feature to demonstrate impact while minimizing risk.

After you've defined your starter project with your manager, start following the product development process to get it done. This process includes understanding the customer problem and goal and working with your engineering and design counterparts to define the product solution.

What Does Success Look Like After 30 Days?

After your first 30 days, you should have:

1. **Built relationships** by meeting 1:1 with the people that you'll be working closely with along with your management chain.
2. **Developed a good understanding** of your customers, company/team mission, strategy/roadmap, and the key metrics that are driving your business.
3. **Found gaps to fill** by helping a few teammates take care of work that they don't want to do themselves.
4. **Defined a starter project** with your manager and started working with stakeholders to get it shipped.

28

INTERVIEW: DAVID WEEKLY

David is the CEO of Medcorder, an app that allows patients to record and share physician consults with their families to make better medical decisions together. Previously, David was a product lead at Google, where he sat on hiring committees and helped Googlers transition to PM internally. In this interview, David provides a lot of great advice about the Google PM hiring process.

Can you talk about your experience at Google?

Sure! At Google, I was the head of product for datacenter software, a team of more than 100 engineers that manages and maintains the software for Google's data centers. I was also actively involved in Google's product manager hiring process. I helped create Google's level-based rubrics for hiring PMs, served on the PM hiring committee and created a "Path to Product Manager" course taken by almost 2,000 Googlers.

Are a lot of Google employees interested in becoming a product manager?

Yes! When I started the "Path to Product Manager" course, I thought that 20 people would sign up. Instead, more than 300 people attended the course in its first run. I think there's a lot of interest in PM roles at Google and other companies.

So how easy is it to transition to product manager from another role at Google?

It's not easy. For many Googlers who transitioned internally, it took many years and multiple failed interview rounds. On the one hand, working at Google means you can ask for mentorship from other Google PMs and browse internal resources. On the other hand, interviewers generally have a higher bar for internal candidates.

What criteria does Google use to evaluate PM candidates?

Google looks for several traits when evaluating PM candidates:

1. **Analytical:** Can you effectively use data to make decisions?
2. **Comprehensive:** Can you approach problems in a structured way? For example, do you focus on end-user pain points first? Do you cover all the bases without "ratholing" on details?
3. **Technical:** Can you understand which parts of the product are feasible to implement and which parts are not? Can you explain complex technical systems clearly?
4. **Communication:** Do you talk through your thinking out loud? Do you refine your thinking based on the interviewer's feedback? Can you get others excited about your ideas? Are they clear?
5. **Creativity:** Do you go breadth-first to brainstorm a lot of ideas before diving into details? Do you come up with unique ideas and solutions that the interviewer didn't think about? Can you usefully reframe problems and even push back on the question to get to a better answer?
6. **Culture:** Are you excited about the job opportunity and intellectually curious?

Can you describe the technical interview in more detail?

For the technical interview, your goal is to avoid provoking an allergic reaction from the engineer who is conducting the interview. Engineers really don't like it when you pretend to know something you don't, so don't try to ad lib or fake something you don't know.

Of course, if you don't know anything that's not a good sign either. You need to spend time studying technical interview questions and show that you can reason from first principles. For example, if I ask you what happens when you type a URL into your browser, you should be able to walk through each step in detail. It's OK if you know more about one part of a problem than another; you can (and should!) guide the interview to showcase the areas where you've gone into more depth.

How does the Google hiring committee work?

The Google hiring committee reviews the feedback from your interviewers and makes a hiring decision. To avoid bias, none of your interviewers are part of your hiring committee.

Candidates who get hired tend to provoke strong reactions in interviewers. For example, if two interviewers say you're one of the best candidates they've ever seen but one interviewer wanted to pass, you actually have a lot better odds than if every interviewer said "lean hire" which is basically "I wouldn't be offended if this person worked at Google but I wouldn't fight to have them on *my* team." You need to turn at least two of your interviewers into fierce advocates for you to join the company.

What's it like being a product manager at Google?

On the one hand, it is great that you're surrounded by really smart people and have the opportunity to work on a wide variety of interesting products. However, Google is an engineering-driven culture so you need to prove your value as a product manager. Don't expect people to revere you or by default look to you for answers. Google is also a really large company so sometimes there are factors that are outside of your control (e.g. your project gets canceled because of a department or company-wide reorganization). Good product managers at Google not only need to master the core PM skills but also be able to effectively manage upward and navigate the organization.

Can you talk about what made you decide to leave Google and start Medcorder?

While I enjoyed my time at Google, I also identify as an entrepreneur. I decided to leave Google because I wanted to tackle a problem that was close to my heart.

Having lost both of my parents to cancer, I created Medcorder to help people like myself take better care of ailing parents and family members from afar. Medcorder allows patients to securely record conversations with their doctor and share them with family and friends so that they can make effective decisions together. We'd like to become a powerful tool for patients and their families to optimize coordination, communication, and outcomes.

Any closing tips for aspiring and new product managers?

Yes, I have a few things that I strongly believe in:

1. **Whether you're interviewing for a PM job or talking to your engineers about a product, always start with the customer problem.** Talk about a pain point that your customer faces and how badly it's broken. It's usually the least objectionable part and it's important to align on the problem before talking about the solution. If people don't understand or believe the pain point, then you need to get other surface area contact with more customers.
2. **Don't get discouraged if you fail a few PM interviews.** A place like Google gets far more excellent applicants than there are available roles to fill, which means that the process knowingly discards a lot of really fantastic folks. (Boo!) Much of it will come down to the people selected to interview you

and the personal chemistry you happen to strike with them. Don't beat yourself up if things don't work out; I failed my first several Google interviews decades ago!

3. **As a PM, just launching your product isn't good enough.** The most important part is learning from your launch and iterating from there.

4. **Learn to leverage your strengths.** If you're really good at a few things, spend time to become unbelievably good at them. Sometimes there could be a critical weakness that's holding you back that you need to work on, but often I've found that my weakness gaps can be filled by other people on my team. Remember, even Olympians have coaches. Don't be afraid to find a mentor even for the things that you're good at.

29

INTERVIEW: JEFF FENG

Jeff is the product lead of data at Airbnb and also helps manage Airbnb's PM hiring process. In this interview, Jeff talks about his journey to PM, what Airbnb looks for when hiring PMs, and what a machine learning PM does.

What do you do at Airbnb?

At Airbnb, I lead the data platform product team. Our team's mission is to build leverage for Airbnb through trustworthy data. We work on the machine learning and experimentation platform that Airbnb uses to run A/B tests and train machine learning models. We also work on improving the company's core data infrastructure.

Product Management Principles

What guiding principles do you think define good product managers?

There are three principles that I think all good PMs should follow:

First, product managers are ultimately responsible for the success or failure of a product—full stop. PMs who take ownership will naturally focus their attention on the most important area to be addressed. There is no task that's too trivial for a PM, whether that's building the roadmap, hiring engineers, or addressing user complaints.

Second, product managers are the curator of great ideas. Many PMs see themselves as being the source of great product ideas, however, I believe that's a dangerous mindset. Great ideas come from all directions whether it is engineers, users or customer support. It's the role of a PM to curate and source the best ideas. Doing so switches the mindset of pushing their ideas to pulling the best ideas.

Finally, product managers are responsible for the pace and quality of decision making. A fallacy is that "PMs are the CEO of the product" or that PMs "call the shots." A great PM rarely ever calls the shots and makes the ultimate decision because it disempowers the rest of their team in the long run. Rather, great PMs will lead the team to make the right decision at the right time.

Can you give me an example of a tough situation that you faced in the past?

When I first started at Airbnb, I was focused on building our first open-source data visualization tool. For our initial release, we wanted to combine a SQL editor with data visualization features.

The initial reception for the tool was positive, especially from technical users who were more comfortable with SQL. As people became more dependent on the tool however, their expectations for quality and performance increased. Six months after launch, we were receiving a lot of negative user feedback about poor performance. Even a single chart took a long time to render. The problem was, many other Airbnb teams were relying on the tool for their product dashboards. You can imagine how other PMs felt when it took longer and longer for them to access their product metrics.

I realized that I had to take ownership of the problem. I sent an organization-wide e-mail talking about the next steps and shared the issue in different product reviews and leadership discussions.

We spent many months improving latency and performance after that. My takeaway from this experience is that people appreciate it when you acknowledge the problem and take ownership of finding a solution.

Data Product Management

What do data product managers do? What skills do they need?

I think there are three types of data PMs:

- Analytics and experimentation: Analytics and experimentation PMs make data-informed decisions when building products. They typically run a lot of A/B tests to prove or disprove their product hypothesis. Examples of this include a PM for the market intelligence team at Airbnb or a growth PM for a game studio. A great understanding of SQL and statistics can help these PMs excel.
- Machine learning: These PMs can frame a machine learning problem and guide a team toward a solution. They must be able to articulate the user needs, determine whether a ML model is needed or whether simple business rules could suffice, understand whether labeled data already exists (and if not, how to obtain it), and ensure that the team is optimizing for the right objective function that's aligned to the business goal. Having a base-level understanding of how machine learning works and common terminology (e.g. accuracy, precision, recall) helps.
- Data platform: Data Platform PMs are extremely deep in technology and data infrastructure. They understand Hive, HDFS, Spark and other big data technologies as well as the full life-cycle of data including logging, ingestion, data processing, and data visualization.

Can you describe machine learning at a high level?

Sure. Supervised machine learning is an approach of building systems that can make accurate and useful predictions on data that's never been seen before. Typically, it requires training a model on a clean set of labeled data and using a combination of features (an input variable) to create the best model.

As a simple analogy, let's imagine you're trying to help a baby identify if an animal is a cat or not. You can show the baby pictures of cats and other animals or ask her to look for a tail, fur, two eyes, or the sound of "meow." The more data points you can correctly label for the baby (cat / not a cat) the more likely the baby can accurately predict if an animal is a cat in that moment and in the future.

How does Airbnb use machine learning?

Airbnb uses machine learning throughout the product experience. Here are some examples:

- Search ranking: Given a user who's searching on our platform, what are the most relevant listings that we should display?
- Smart pricing: Given the listing's location, other listings in the area, and other features, what is the optimal price for which the host should list his house?
- Listing image classification: Given a listing image, what type of image is it (e.g. is it a bedroom, living room, kitchen, bathroom, etc.)?
- Support ticket routing: Given a support issue, should we route it to an internal high-cost support channel or an external low-cost support channel?

You can read more about how we use machine learning on our engineering blog.

How can one pick up machine learning skills?

There are many great online resources. My favorites include:

1. https://developers.google.com/machine-learning/crash-course/
2. https://www.coursera.org/learn/machine-learning
3. https://www.coursera.org/specializations/deep-learning
4. https://www.udacity.com/learn/machinelearning

Transitioning to Product Management

How did you become a product manager?

I transitioned to product management after working as a consultant at McKinsey for two years. Consultants, like PMs, need to be problem solvers, strong communicators, and adept at handling ambiguity.

Despite being a consultant for two years and having an MBA from MIT, I still had to convince PM hiring managers that I could do the job with minimal product experience. It took at least three months for me to land any PM offer.

What did you do during those three months?

I spent those three months studying PM interview questions and reading blogs. I also looked at different products and asked myself what I liked and disliked about them. I tried to apply the frameworks that I picked up from reading PM books and blogs to assess these products.

Great, and what was your first PM job?

My first PM job was at Tableau software as a product manager focused on partner integrations. I think I landed this job because I had strong partnership experience from consulting and technical expertise dating back to my time working as a Ph.D. candidate at MIT.

In other words, I was able to transition because there were unique aspects of my background that was attractive to the team at Tableau.

Do you have any advice for people who are trying to land their first product manager job?

Yes, try to approach the process of landing your first PM job with the mindset of a product manager.

Start with the end goal of where you want to be 3-5 years from now and work backward from that. For example, do you want to help scale products or build a new product from scratch? Do you want to start your own company 3-5 years from now or work as a PM in a large company?

Next, take a hard look at what you bring to the table. The hardest thing about landing your first PM role is convincing hiring managers that you have high potential despite minimal experience shipping a product. If you're not transferring internally, take a hard assessment of your strengths and weaknesses, and think about why the hiring manager may choose you over someone with more experience.

Try to find PM jobs where you can leverage your unique strengths and expertise.

Airbnb's Product Management Hiring Process

You helped define Airbnb's PM hiring process. Can you explain what Airbnb looks for in PMs?

Sure, Airbnb looks for six attributes in evaluating which PMs to hire. We use these same six attributes to evaluate PMs on the job as well:

1. Product Sense
2. Product Execution
3. Leadership
4. Communication
5. Collaboration

6. Domain Fit

We also look for PMs who have a growth mindset—people who are always looking to learn and improve.

What is Airbnb's interview process like?

Candidates will typically have 1-2 phone screens followed by a full day onsite consisting of a presentation based on a prompt (typically a take-home assignment that they can prepare ahead of time), 3 PM interviews, 2 cross-functional interviews (e.g. engineering, design, analytics) and 2 core values interviews.

Wow, that sounds intense. How can a candidate prepare for the interviews?

Here's my advice for preparing for Airbnb's product interviews, but I think it can be generalized to PM interviews overall as well.

First, as a PM candidate, you should understand Airbnb's products and write down what you think the user pain points, goals/metrics, and key features are. Think through how you would improve our products in the short-term and also what the long-term vision is. Of course, the best way to understand our products is to stay in an Airbnb or book an experience. Candidates who use our products and understand our company mission well usually stand out in the interview process. Here are some questions to help you think about our products:

1. What do you like or dislike about our products as a user?
2. What features would you add or remove if you were the PM of this product?
3. How would you measure success?
4. What are the big opportunities for Airbnb?

Second, you should reflect on Airbnb's values and how your experience might be relevant. Here are the values that we look for in candidates:

1. Champion the mission: Prioritize work that advances the mission and positively impacts the community. Build with the long-term in mind.
2. Be a host: Care for others, make them feel like they belong, and encourage others to participate to their fullest. Listen, communicate openly, and set clear expectations.
3. Embrace the adventure: Be curious, ask for help, and demonstrate an ability to grow. Own and learn from mistakes. Bring joy and optimism to work.
4. Be a cereal entrepreneur: Be bold and apply original thinking. Imagine the ideal outcome and be resourceful to make that outcome a reality.

Any parting words of wisdom for aspiring product managers?

Talk to as many existing PMs as you can to understand what people love about the job. Make sure these reasons resonate with you—you want to become a PM for the right reasons.

To me, being a PM is not about being the CEO or the person who calls the shots. PMs are responsible for the success or failure of a product and trying to fill any gaps on the team. People who want to be PM should be excited about building products and leading without authority.

When I'm hiring product managers, the two biggest things that I look for are a growth mindset and leadership skills. To develop a growth mindset, you should always be hungry to get more feedback to help you grow personally. For leadership, you should see problems not as barriers but as opportunities to excel. You should be someone who can raise the status quo instead of just accepting how things work today. I look for people who can rally a team together and whom others are willing to put their trust.

EPILOGUE

There are two defining moments in my product management career so far.

The first moment is after I failed the Facebook PM interview loop twice in a row. Back then, I was ready to give up. I started to think: "Maybe I just don't have the right skills to be a product manager, maybe I should be happy to be in my current job." But a good friend told me: If this is your goal, then you can't give up. You're just going to have to keep trying because otherwise, you're not going to be happy. And if you're not satisfied, you're not going to succeed in your current job either." That pushed me to look for product roles externally, and with persistence, I was able to land an offer.

The second moment is after I received a negative performance review a year into my journey as a new PM. That review forced me to take a hard look at myself. I realized that I needed to be more patient and to focus more on building relationships instead of just getting things done.

Maybe you've also experienced moments like above. Maybe you've been trying to become a product manager for a while but have failed multiple job interviews. Or maybe you're a few years into your PM journey and are not progressing as fast as you'd like.

Everyone experiences setbacks. The difference is how you respond to it. I like this equation from Ray Dalio, the billionaire hedge fund investor:[1]

$$Pain + Reflection = Progress$$

If you can reflect well on your setbacks, make adjustments, and never give up, then you will make progress toward your goal. And if you make progress, you'll still be in a better spot than you were before, even if you don't reach your goal.

I hope that reading this book has helped you with your product management journey. When you experience pain or failure, I hope you reflect on the PM principles to become a more effective leader. When you're building a product, I hope that you follow the "understand, identify, and execute" product development loop to create products that customers love. Finally, I hope you apply the principles and the product development loop to transitioning to product management and acing your product interviews.

So, never give up and have the courage to go after what you want.

———

IF YOU ENJOYED THIS BOOK, please leave a review on Amazon and visit www.principles.pm to sign up for the book's mailing list. Thank you for reading!

PM PRINCIPLES

1. Take Ownership

Be humble

Control negative emotions

Build relationships

2. Prioritize and Execute

Focus

Communicate your priorities

Do whatever it takes

3. Start with Why

Obsess about the customer problem

Communicate why constantly

Keep it simple

4. Find the Truth

Seek knowledgeable people

Balance decision quality with decision speed

Disagree and commit

5. Be Radically Transparent

Care personally

Challenge directly

Empower others

6. Be Honest with Yourself

Set clear goals

Reflect often

Seek feedback from others

REFERENCES

5. Be Radically Transparent

1. Kim Scott (March 2017). *Radical Candor: How to Get What You Want by Saying What You Mean*. New York, NY: St Martin's Press.

10. Understanding the Customer Problem

1. Jeff Bezos (April 2017). 2016 Letter to Shareholders. Retrieved from https://blog.aboutamazon.com/company-news/2016-letter-to-shareholders

12. Mission, Vision, and Strategy

1. Jeff Bezos (November 2017). Kindle at 10. Retrieved from https://blog.aboutamazon.com/devices/kindle-at-10-reading-just-keeps-getting-better
2. Richard Rumelt (2011). *Good Strategy / Bad Strategy*. New York, NY: Random House.
3. Elon Musk (August 2006). The Secret Tesla Master Plan. Retrieved from https://www.tesla.com/blog/secret-tesla-motors-master-plan-just-between-you-and-me

13. Building a Product Roadmap

1. Andy S. Grove (2015). *High Output Management*. New York, NY: Vintage Books.

14. Defining Product Requirements

1. To learn more about Amazon Go, visit https://www.amazon.com/go.

15. Great Project Management

1. Dogfood means testing your product internally to find bugs and issues before launch.

16. Effective Communication

1. William Strunk Jr (1979). *The Elements of Style*. Needham Heights, MA: Pearson.

20. Preparing for the Transition

1. Steve Jobs (1994). Steve Jobs on Failure. Retrieved from https://www.youtube.com/watch?v=zkTfoLmDqKI

21. Making the Transition

1. Jim Carrey (May 2014). Jim Carrey's Commencement Address at the 2014 MUM Graduation. Retrieved from https://www.youtube.com/watch?v=V80-gPkpH6M
2. Chris Hadfield (March 2013). Chris Hadfield on how you can achieve your goals. Retrieved from https://www.youtube.com/watch?v=eGrzo4IvXyg

22. Finding the Right Company

1. https://blog.wealthfront.com/career-launching-companies-list/

Epilogue

1. Ray Dalio (2017). *Principles.* New York, NY: Simon & Schuster.

ABOUT THE AUTHOR

Peter Yang has worked in product management and product marketing roles at companies such as Amazon, Twitter, Facebook, and Microsoft. Outside of work, Peter runs training and mentorship courses to help the next generation of PMs succeed. He has an MBA from MIT and a Bachelors from Brown University.

Peter can be found on:

Twitter: https://twitter.com/petergyang

LinkedIn: https://www.linkedin.com/in/yangpeter/

Made in the USA
Middletown, DE
18 May 2020